CALIFORNIA
WINE
COUNTRY

A SUNSET FIELD GUIDE

by
Peter Fish and Sara Schneider

CONTENTS

INTRODUCTION | 4

USING THIS BOOK | 6

NAPA | 8

Cool Carneros in the south, Rutherford and Yountville in the valley's heart, and St. Helena and Calistoga to the north

SONOMA | 34

A laid-back land of valleys, from Sonoma to Alexander to Dry Creek to Russian River

MENDOCINO | 60

Old vines grow in the Anderson Valley; newer ones are bearing fruit along Highway 101 between Hopland and Redwood Vallley

10 9 8 7 6 5 4 3 2 1

First Printing March 2007

Copyright © 2007 by Sunset Publishing Corporation, Menlo Park, CA 94025

Illustrations Copyright © 2006 by Michael Schwab

Maps: Eureka Cartography, Berkeley, CA; 510/845-MAPS; www.maps-eureka.com

Photograph of Karen MacNeil: Michael Weschler

ISBN-13: 978-0-376-06947-4

ISBN-10: 0-376-06947-3

Library of Congress Control Number: 2006932573

Printed in China

LAKE | 72
This growing region surrounds a jewel of a lake

SIERRA | 76
El Dorado, Amador, and Calaveras counties offer Gold Rush history and killer Zin

SANTA CRUZ | 90
The mountains north of this surf-happy university town harbor secret vineyards

MONTEREY | 102
Tour the peninsula, explore the wineries of Carmel Valley, and detour north to San Benito County for wine discoveries

SAN LUIS OBISPO | 116
Paso Robles is arguably the hottest wine region in the state; Edna Valley is one of the oldest

SANTA BARBARA | 130
Go to the Santa Rita Hills and the Santa Maria Valley for Pinot Noir, and to Santa Ynez Valley for just about everything

TEMECULA | 146
Golf and grapes coexist just minutes from millions of Southern Californians

BAJA | 150
A new wine region is blossoming north of Ensenada and south of Tecate

GLOSSARY | 156

WINE CLUBS | 158

INDEX | 160

SUNSET BOOKS

VICE PRESIDENT, GENERAL MANAGER:
Richard A. Smeby

VICE PRESIDENT, EDITORIAL DIRECTOR:
Bob Doyle

DIRECTOR OF OPERATIONS:
Rosann Sutherland

MARKETING MANAGER: Linda Barker

ART DIRECTOR: Vasken Guiragossian

SPECIAL SALES: Brad Moses

STAFF FOR THIS BOOK

SENIOR EDITOR: Ben Marks

ART DIRECTOR: Alice Rogers

PREPRESS COORDINATOR:
Eligio Hernández

COPY EDITOR: Cynthia Rubin

PRODUCTION SPECIALIST:
Linda M. Bouchard

PROOFREADER/INDEXER:
Jennifer Block Martin

INTERN: Esther Kim

ACKNOWLEDGMENTS

We would like to extend special thanks to Sunset *magazine writers and editors David C. Becker, Matthew Jaffe, Lisa Taggart, and Amy Wolf for their contributions. Thanks also to* Sunset's *editor-in-chief, Katie Tamony. Finally, a big thank you to Lory Day.*

For additional copies of *California Wine Country* or any other Sunset book, visit us at www.sunsetbooks.com or call 1-800-526-5111.

INTRODUCTION

CALIFORNIA IS WINE'S CAMELOT—a place of high ideals, majestic beauty, contagious excitement, and the powerful belief that everything good is deliciously possible. Of all of the wine regions of the world, none, I think, possesses a spirit that's quite as remarkable, as exuberant. You can sense it in the air. You can even taste it in the wines.

When I first began visiting the California wine country in the early 1970s, places such as the Napa Valley, Sonoma County, and certainly the entire Central Coast had a distinct pioneering feel. Visitors like me were often lost, hungry, or both since restaurants were scarce and guides like this one nonexistent. (The leading wine book at the time, Hugh Johnson's *World Atlas of Wine*, had 72 pages devoted to France; five to California.) Looking back, I'd say it's a testament to the love vintners have for their land that the California wine country has maintained its ruralness and serenity while becoming sophisticated and worldly at the same time.

If there was a turning point for the California wine industry, a moment when it vaulted onto the world wine scene, it was in 1976 when a tasting now known as the Judgment of Paris was staged by English wine expert Steven Spurrier. The blind tasting included such stellar Bordeaux as Château Haut-Brion and Château Mouton-Rothschild, as well as top-ranked Burgundies like Domaine Ramonet-Prudhon Bâtard Montrachet and Joseph Drouhin Beaune Clos des Mouches. All the California labels in the tasting were then unknowns. They included Ridge, Stag's Leap Wine Cellars, and Freemark Abbey for the Cabernet Sauvignons and Chateau Montelena and Chalone among the Chardonnays.

As Mr. Spurrier has recounted many times since, the nine French judges were confident—indeed, cocksure—that the renowned Bordeaux and Burgundies would come out on top. Alas, when the scores were counted, the judges were stunned to learn they had voted the 1973 Stag's Leap Wine Cellars Cabernet Sauvignon and Chateau Montelena Chardonnay the best wines of the tasting. Every major newspaper and news magazine, from *Le Monde* to *Time*, carried the astonishing results.

Recently, in the spring of 2006, Mr. Spurrier reenacted the Judgment of Paris with a blind tasting of reds. For years, critics had asserted that California wines had an undisputed sexiness when they were *young*. This time around, of course, each of the wines was 30 years older. Would older California wines stand up against older Bordeaux and Burgundy?

I took part in the reenactment. The room was more silent than a cathedral as we tasters concentrated on the wines. In the end, Ridge Monte Bello Cabernet Sauvignon came in first, Stag's Leap Wine Cellars Cabernet Sauvignon second, and Heitz Cellars and Mayacamas tied for third place. The top-scoring Bordeaux, Château Mouton-Rothschild, came in sixth.

And so, this book comes at the perfect time. California is poised on the threshold of a new golden era. Its wines are reaching heights of quality undreamed of just a generation ago. For their part, California's ever-innovative winemakers, inspired by fascinating Spanish, German, Italian, and French grapes, are now working with dozens of new grape varieties. And of course the number of wineries continues to climb. At this writing, there are some 2,000 wineries in California; in 1970, there were just 240. Helping you navigate all this action, and guiding you to the best tasting rooms, restaurants, and attractions in the California wine country, is what this book is all about.

Finally, a few words about the book's coauthors, Sara Schneider and Peter Fish. I've tasted hundreds of wines with Sara, who's a colleague and friend, and Peter appears determined to leave no part of California undiscovered. As a result of their passionate research, this guide has a spirit of its own: It says: *Use me.* I know my own copy will in short order look happily road-weary and worn. And it will probably have a few red wine stains to boot.

Karen MacNeil

USING THIS BOOK

The wineries and travel destinations listed in *California Wine Country* have been organized into geographic regions and areas. In some cases these regions follow county lines; in other cases they don't. Appellations are referred to throughout the book, but we have not grouped wineries strictly by appellation since that's probably not how you'll plan a visit to most regions and areas.

· · · · · · ·

Each region's description begins with an introductory essay, followed by listings for **Wineries** and **Things to Do,** as well as suggestions for **Where to Eat** and **Places to Stay.**

· · · · · · ·

Phone numbers and URLs of local

for more info: Amador Vintners' Association: 888/655-8614; amadorwine.com   83

visitor and vintner associations can be found in the **for more info** bars at the bottom of many pages.

· · · · · · ·

To help you find the wineries listed in *California Wine Country,* all winery listings are numbered so they can be located on corresponding maps.

15 | SCHRAMSBERG VINEYARDS

History was made here in 1965, when Jack and Jamie Davies bough^... winery (second-oldest in the valley, founded by German immi... Schram in 1862) and were the first in the country to make spa... you a look at a mind-boggling 2 million bottles of bubble... caves dug out at the turn of the last century, plus interest... dosage, and other sparkling wine-making techniques.

1400 Schramsberg Road, Calistoga | 800/877-3623
schramsberg.com

· · · · · · ·

Some regions have dozens of wineries, which can make choosing one winery over another a daunting task. For at-a-glance help in deciding which ones to visit, look for **Suggested Routes** and **Favorites & Discoveries.**

SUGGESTED ROUTES

☆ FOXEN CANYON *Explore the wineries of Santa Maria Valley, then follow Foxen Canyon Road south to Santa Ynez*

☆ SANTA RITA HILLS *Begin in Buell... ...t on Highway 246 to Lompoc, then return via sceni... lamos*

☆ SANTA YNEZ TRIANGLE *Highway 154 between S... ...between Los Olivos and...*

FAVORITES & DISCOVERIES ☆ SANTA YNEZ

...ESS PARKER WINERY AND VINEYARD *Dependable everyday ...ing wine, with a tourist-friendly tasting room and store*

...MESA WINERY AND VINEYARD *Where some of the area's ...st famous winemakers learned their craft*

...NDREW MURRAY VINEYARDS *Longtime valley grower's winery is worth seeking out*

...STOLPMAN *Represents a new generation of winemakers giving travelers a reason to visit Solvang besides Danish pastry*

Finally, **Spotlights** have been sprinkled throughout the book to give you more information on key people, places, and trends in a particular region.

WINE TASTING

Lest it go without saying, don't drink and drive. If you are tasting your way through a wine region, be sure to pace yourself. Better yet, take turns behind the wheel: Give the keys to one of your traveling companions on your first day of touring, then take over driving duties the next.

The wineries listed in *California Wine Country* all have regular tasting hours unless otherwise stated (look for the words "call for appointment" next to a winery's phone number). For some wineries regular hours only pertain to weekends, while still others change their hours depending on the season—make it the navigator's job to call ahead while you're on the road, or check winery websites before heading out.

Prices charged at tasting rooms range from free to $5 for a flight of a winery's current releases to $10 for a logo'ed glass (which you keep and use for tasting) to $50 for special wine-and-food pairings. You are not expected to buy anything when you visit a tasting room and, in fact, the bottle prices at most wineries are higher than at your local BevMo, but the tasting fee, or a portion of it in the case of a wine-and-food pairing, is often applied to any purchase you make at the end of your tasting. The biggest advantage of tasting at a winery, beyond the conviviality of the experience, is the opportunity to sample and purchase so-called library wines that are not available anywhere else.

CONTACT US

If you'd like to suggest a winery, restaurant, or place to stay for possible inclusion in a future edition of *California Wine Country*, please send an email to calwine@sunset.com.

NAPA

FOR MOST OF THE WORLD, "NAPA VALLEY" is shorthand for all California wines, in the same way that Hollywood means American movies. It's home to some of California's grandest wineries—towering, Germanic Beringer; stately Rubicon Estate—as well as its most jaw-droppingly extravagant contemporary ones—Darioush, a Persian-style palace; Clos Pegase, Babylon as interpreted by architect Michael Graves. This is the sort of place where an acre of good vineyard land runs $120,000, where tickets for two to the Napa Valley Wine Auction go for $7,500, where a cult Cabernet can fetch $500 a bottle.

Roughly 30 miles long and five miles wide, the valley and the bench-lands and mountain peaks that surround it contain, at last count, 400 wineries. Their right to the "Napa Valley" moniker on their labels gives every bottle a pedigree—and corresponding price tag.

The seeds of the valley's current golden age were planted in the late 1800s, when General George Yount presented his granddaughter Elizabeth and soon-to-be-husband, Thomas Rutherford, with about 1,000 acres of land. The vineyards Rutherford cultivated became the estates of Inglenook (now Rubicon Estate) and Beaulieu Vineyard (known as BV).

Along with these two wineries, two men—André Tchelistcheff and Robert Mondavi—get much of the credit for bringing Napa Valley wine-making up to world-class standards, as well as spreading the word. Tchelistcheff enters the picture in 1937, when BV founder Georges de Latour had the insight to import the Russian winemaker after the pall of Prohibition. Tchelistcheff mentored generations of winemakers, including current BV winemaker Jeffrey Stambor. For his part, Robert Mondavi

Continues page 10 >

SUGGESTED ROUTES

☆ **SOUTH VALLEY ART**
Start at the di Rosa Preserve, whose collection of Bay Area art surpasses SFMOMA's, then head to Artesa to see what the artist in residence has been up to. Continue on to Hess Collection for contemporary paintings and sculpture.

☆ **ST. HELENA HIGHWAY** Great wineries along the valley's main drag, from south to north, include Cardinale, Mondavi, St. Supéry, Rubicon Estate, Beaulieu, Grgich Hills, Heitz, Beringer, and Markham.

☆ **SILVERADO TRAIL**
The valley's eastside road has less traffic. Stellar wineries include (south to north) Clos du Val, Stag's Leap Wine Cellars, Robert Sinskey, Joseph Phelps, and Cuvaison.

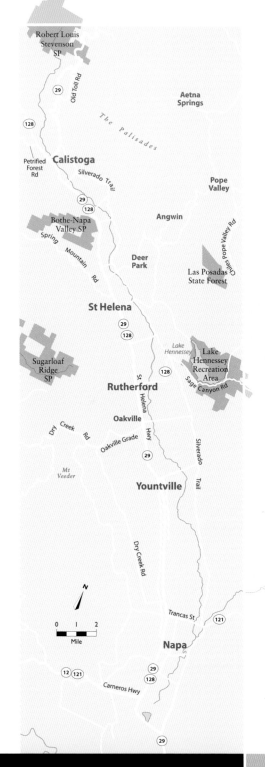

Robert Louis Stevenson SP

29

128

The Palisades

Aetna Springs

Old Toll Rd

Petrified Forest Rd

Calistoga

Silverado Trail

Pope Valley

29

128

Bothe-Napa Valley SP

Angwin

Chiles Pope Valley Rd

Spring Mountain Rd

Deer Park

Las Posadas State Forest

St Helena

29

128

Sugarloaf Ridge SP

Lake Hennessey

Lake Hennessey Recreation Area

128

Sage Canyon Rd

Rutherford

St Helena Hwy

Dry Creek Rd

Oakville

Oakville Grade

Silverado Trail

29

Mt Veeder

Yountville

N

Dry Creek Rd

0   1   2
Mile

Trancas St

121

12 121

29

128

Carneros Hwy

Napa

29

has been a tireless ambassador for California wine. Along the way he's built countless bridges, such as his partnership with Bordeaux's Baroness Philippine de Rothschild to produce a Napa Valley version of a grand cru–level Cabernet blend: Opus One.

Indeed, Napa wines have been acknowledged to be on par with their French counterparts since their triumphs over red Bordeaux and white Burgundies at the 1976 Judgment of Paris tasting. Today, the reputation of the region rides largely on one grape: Cabernet Sauvignon. Hundreds of grape varieties were planted in the valley's early years, and a few now make some pretty great wine—Merlot and other Bordeaux varieties especially, plus some Zinfandel, Sauvignon Blanc, and, in the cool-weather Carneros District, Chardonnay. But in Napa, Cab is king.

The heart of the valley, around Rutherford and Oakville, produces some of the most sought-after Cabs in the world—meaty, lush, layered, wonderful. Oakville Cross Road is flanked by wineries with cult potential: Rudd, Groth, PlumpJack, Harlan, Screaming Eagle. Attention is increasingly focused on the benchlands that lie against the Mayacamas to the west and the Vaca Range to the east. Greatness has even been found in the mountains—Veeder, Diamond, Spring, and Howell.

Napa Valley, an American Viticultural Area, also known as an appellation or AVA, is carved into more than a dozen smaller appellations. The process of establishing boundaries is as political as you can imagine, since the word "Rutherford" on a bottle immediately raises its price. But for the wine-loving visitor, tasting across the AVAs of Napa Valley—searching for traces of "Rutherford dust"—just shouldn't be missed.

Not surprisingly, along with all this great wine has come equally impressive cuisine. Tiny Yountville boasts an embarrassment of world-class restaurants, while St. Helena, possibly the most glamorous small town in the country, is nearly as rich in dining options. The best of the valley resorts are likewise in a class by themselves. To watch the sunset from a deck at Auberge du Soleil or play a round of croquet at Meadowood is to experience la dolce vita, Northern California style.

Given all these choices, what's a Napa visitor do? For starters, relax. For all its opulent tasting rooms and five-star prix-fixe menus, this is still a region of rural character that likes to please its visitors.

Strategy is key. The valley can be crowded on weekends from spring through autumn (although it's typically a good-natured crowd). When the hall-of-fame march of wineries up the St. Helena Highway (State 29) or Silverado Trail gets too jammed, head to the backroads, where the two-lane asphalt cruises like a dream past plantings of Cabernet and Zinfandel. If you want the place more to yourself, visit on a weekday; if you want it really to yourself, visit in winter, when the vineyards and oaks take on a stark, skeletal beauty.

The trick in Napa, frankly, is to assume you'll be back. Take your time; don't try to see everything all at once. Grab a loaf of good bread and an untried bottle of Napa Valley wine, find a picnic spot, spread your blanket, and enjoy this very special corner of the world.

SOUTH VALLEY WINERIES

1 | DOMAINE CARNEROS BY TAITTINGER

A replica of the French Taittinger family's 17th-century stone château in Champagne, Domaine Carneros has a grand terrace for sipping the good bubbly it makes. Splurge on a bottle of Le Rêve. President and winemaker Eileen Crane also produces small lots of still Pinot Noir that are only available at the winery.

1240 Duhig Road, Napa | 707/257-0101 | domaine.com

2 | ACACIA VINEYARD

From the grounds of Acacia Vineyard, you can literally see why the Carneros District is the perfect place for cold-weather-loving Pinot Noir and Chardonnay—cooling San Pablo Bay lies just 2 miles away. Acacia was an early shaper of Carneros Pinot style and is still pushing the boundaries.

2750 Las Amigas Road, Napa | 877/226-1700 (call for appointment) | acaciavineyard.com

3 | ARTESA VINEYARDS & WINERY

This intriguing, modern structure is seemingly built underground, with grass growing up the building's sloping walls. The paradoxically airy visitor center includes a sculpture garden, a pair of mini museums devoted to local geology and historical winemaking tools, and a large tasting room and terrace. Artesa Pinots and Chardonnays are classic Carneros wines.

1345 Henry Road, Napa | 707/224-1668 | artesawinery.com

4 | ETUDE WINES

Etude's Pinot Noirs go to the core of Carneros quality, and they give longtime grower and Etude founder, Tony Soter, a perfect "vehicle for practicing the craft of winemaking." The focus in this large stone edifice, though, is on that craft more than on visitors, but try dropping in—if it fits into the staff's schedule, you can tour and taste.

1250 Cuttings Wharf Road, Napa | 707/257-5300 (call for appointment) | etudewines.com

5 | THE HESS COLLECTION WINERY

The "collection" in the name might refer to the art in the multilevel gallery that holds the winery, founded by Donald Hess of Swiss bottled-water fame, or to the lines of wines it produces. The best of the bunch is the Cabernet whose grapes grow on Mt. Veeder.

4411 Redwood Road, Napa | 707/255-1144 | hesscollection.com

6 | MAYACAMAS

Located practically at the top of Mt. Veeder, just this side of the Sonoma County line, this 5,000-cases-a-year winery specializes in Cabernet Sauvignon (Mayacamas tied for third in the 2006 replay of the Judgment of Paris) and Chardonnay. Smaller amounts of Savignon Blanc and Pinot Noir are also produced.

1155 Lokoya Road, Napa | 707/224-4030 (call for appointment) | mayacamas.com

7 | VINTNER'S COLLECTIVE

Even in a place like Napa, known for palatial wineries and equally grand tasting rooms, there are still winemakers who only focus on the art of making great wine. Vintner's Collective, housed in Napa's oldest stone building, is devoted to the products of some 20 such winemakers. Visit the collective and leave with a bottle that you couldn't find anywhere else.

1245 Main Street, Napa | 707/255-7150 | vintnerscollective.com

8 | LUNA VINEYARDS

At the Napa end of the Silverado Trail, Italianate Luna has joined the local trend of offering high-end "experiences" rather than mere tastings, which in this case means pairing some of Luna's upper-tier wines with cheeses, pâtés, and the like. The wines themselves include some single Italian varieties, a few rather wild blends ("Canto," a mix of Sangiovese, Merlot, Cabernet Sauvignon, Cab Franc, *and* Petite Sirah, is Luna's version of a super-Tuscan), and a line of "Arnold Palmer" wines (a collaboration between Luna cofounder Mike Moone and his legendary friend).

2921 Silverado Trail, Napa | 707/255-2474 | lunavineyards.com

9 | DARIOUSH

With this Persian palace, Napa outdoes Napa. "Stunning" is usually an exaggeration; not here. You can spend quite a bit for cheese and wine "experiences" and tours of the whole place, or share the pretty hefty fee for a standard tasting and feel like royalty for an hour.

4240 Silverado Trail, Napa | 707/257-2345 | darioush.com

10 | TREFETHEN

For a refreshing break from heavy Napa reds, visit historic Trefethen, which is known for its Chardonnay—but don't overlook its crisp and beautiful dry Riesling.

1160 Oak Knoll Avenue, Napa | 707/255-7700 | trefethen.com

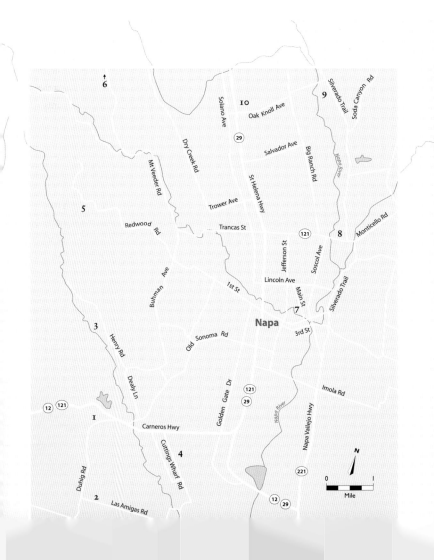

THINGS TO DO

BALLOONING

The combination of altitude, gorgeous scenery, and perhaps a little sparkling wine is a potent one. Napa ballooning companies include Balloons Above the Valley (800/464-6824; balloonrides.com) and Napa Valley Balloons (800/253-2224; napavalleyballoons.com).

COPIA

This $50 million extravaganza, whose official name is the American Center for Wine, Food, and Art, has been undergoing some growing pains, but it still makes a good starting point for a Napa Valley tour. Take a food or wine class (the intro to wine tasting is especially useful), visit the herb gardens, or stroll through galleries filled with food-related exhibits. Copia's restaurant, Julia's Kitchen, offers artful, if not inexpensive, lunches and dinners.

500 First Street, Napa | 707/259-1600 | copia.org

DI ROSA PRESERVE

Ex-newspaperman Rene di Rosa created this 200-acre retreat featuring works by contemporary California artists displayed in a former winery-turned-gallery and outside in the preserve's lovely gardens, olive groves, and even on its 35-acre lake. Visit the Gatehouse Gallery anytime or call to take a tour.

5200 Carneros Highway, Napa | 707/226-5991 | dirosapreserve.org

SPOTLIGHT NAPA'S OXBOW DISTRICT

*Since opening its doors in 2001, **Copia** has been a somewhat lonely outpost in downtown Napa's Oxbow district, at the tip of that ear-shape patch of land surrounded by a radical bend in the Napa River. But Copia is about to get some company. By fall of 2007, **Oxbow Public Market** will open next door. Organic grocer **Long Meadow Ranch** has signed on to be the market's anchor tenant (a wine merchant is one of 20 additional vendors inside and 10 vendors outside), and the building's design features an 8,000-square-foot deck that affords visitors views of the river and the Oxbow Preserve on the other side. Roughly simultaneously, the 12-acre preserve is undergoing a native-plant facelift to ensure that this urban oasis remains a draw for wildlife. And by the end of 2008, the 180-room Riverbend Resort joins the neighborhood.*

DOWNTOWN NAPA

For decades the forgotten stepsister to more famous up-valley towns, downtown Napa has livened up considerably, with historic buildings renovated and an infusion of restaurants, galleries, and shops. You see it at its best if you visit during an event like Chef's Market, which runs Friday evenings in summer.

napadowntown.com

NAPA RIVER CRUISES

Motor launches take passengers up the sleepy but scenic Napa River, with good views and wildlife along the way.

707/224-9080 | napariveradventures.com

NAPA VALLEY OPERA HOUSE

One of the jewels of downtown Napa, the 1879 Italianate building underwent a lavish renovation—funded in large part by Robert Mondavi and his wife, Margrit—and now houses two jazz and theater venues, the intimate Cafe Theater and the bigger Margrit Biever Mondavi Theatre.

1030 Main Street, Napa | 707/226-7372 | napavalleyoperahouse.org

NAPA VALLEY WINE TRAIN

Vintage railcars carry passengers on food-and-wine-fueled lunch and dinner excursions from Napa to Yountville and back, with stops at a winery or two along the way. Trips last about three hours.

1275 McKinstry Street, Napa | 800/427-4124 | winetrain.com

WHERE TO EAT

ANGÈLE

Classic French-country favorites in a cozy corner by the Napa River. The dining room is casual, with concrete floors and wood beams; the water-view terrace is pleasant, but can get breezy in the evening.

540 Main Street, Napa | 707/252-8115 | angelerestaurant.com

BISTRO DON GIOVANNI

Authentic Italian fare in a setting that shows off the valley thanks to heated outdoor dining. Deep-fried olives are a great wine partner to start with; legendary spaghetti and clams or pork chops with olive oil mashed potatoes follow. The wine list has a $950 Cab on it, but there are also excellent by-the-glass choices.

4110 Howard Lane, Napa | 707/224-3300 | bistrodongiovanni.com

CELADON

Greg Cole, of Cole's Chop House, branches into California and Mediterranean traditions with Asian touches here. Brick walls and banquettes make for a stylish dining room, while a fireplace warms up the patio.

500 Main Street, Suite G, Napa | **707/254-9690** | **celadonnapa.com**

COLE'S CHOP HOUSE.

Rib-eye, porterhouse, New York: At this upscale steakhouse, all the important decisions revolve around beef. The sides are traditional (creamed spinach, onion rings) and the setting—especially the patio—attractively casual.

1122 Main Street, Napa | **707/224-6328** | **coleschophouse.com**

SWEETIE PIE'S

Got a morning yen for strong coffee and rich, delicious muffins and scones? This is the place. Good panini for lunch, sumptuous cakes, and pies, too.

520 Main Street, Napa | **707/257-8817** | **sweetiepies.com**

THE BOUNTY HUNTER

True West for wine lovers: beer-can chicken, ribs, tangy pulled-pork sandwiches, and Grandma's mac 'n' cheese served under last century's pounded-tin ceilings, plus more than 400 bottles available on the shelves and 40 wines by the glass.

975 First Street, Napa | **800/943-9463** | **bountyhunterwine.com**

ZUZU

Mediterranean and Latin American tapas in a warm wood-beamed, tiled space. Many wines listed for less than $30 a bottle, and more than 25 available by the glass.

829 Main Street, Napa | **707/224-8555** | **zuzunapa.com**

PLACES TO STAY

BEAZLEY HOUSE

This imposing brown-shingled Colonial Revival home was one of the Napa Valley's first bed-and-breakfast inns and remains one of its best. 11 rooms from $165.

1910 First Street, Napa | **800/559-1649** | **beazleyhouse.com**

BEST WESTERN ELM HOUSE INN

Pleasant and reasonably priced (for Napa) motel, with big rooms and convenient location near downtown. 22 rooms from $139.

800 California Boulevard, Napa | **707/255-1831** | **bestwestern.com**

CARNEROS INN

The Carneros region came of age when this resort, part of San Francisco Mayor Gavin Newsom's PlumpJack Group, opened. The board-and-batten cottages, which range from 975 to 1,800 square feet, harkens back to the area's agrarian past, but the level of luxury is more *Robb Report* than American Gothic. The three restaurants— the soigné Hilltop Dining Room, the elegantly homespun Boon Fly Cafe, and a new spot called The Farm—are equally ambitious. 86 cottages from $435.

4048 Sonoma Highway, Napa | 888/400-9000 | thecarnerosinn.com

MERITAGE RESORT

About five miles south of Napa, this brand-new spa resort is convenient both to Carneros wineries and to the city of Napa itself. The setting, adjacent to an office park, is businesslike, but the lobby, pool, and guest rooms are suitably sybaritic. 158 rooms from $199.

875 Bordeaux Way, Napa | 866/370-6272 | themeritageresort.com

NAPA RIVER INN

Exposed brick rules in this appealing historic inn—it occupies a portion of an 1884 mill—on the edge of downtown and on the banks of the Napa River. 66 rooms and suites from $199.

500 Main Street, Napa | 707/251-8500 | napariverinn.com

POETRY INN

High-end, luxurious inn set in the valley's Stags Leap District. The guest rooms and the views are as impressive as the wine collection in the cellar. 5 rooms from $575.

6380 Silverado Trail, Napa | 707/944-0646 | poetryinn.com

RIVER TERRACE INN

Modern Craftsman-style lodging and a convenient location near Copia and the Napa Wine Train depot. 106 guest rooms from $199.

1600 Soscol Avenue, Napa | 866/627-2386 | riverterraceinn.com

SILVERADO COUNTRY CLUB RESORT

Wine lovers and golf aficionados flock to this venerable resort, which features not one but two Robert Trent Jones courses and easy access to valley wineries. The 16,000-square-foot Spa at Silverado satisfies another constituency—ask about the Spa Girl package, which includes a suite with a fireplace, a 50-minute treatment, and full use of the spa. 280 rooms from $160.

1600 Atlas Peak Road, Napa | 800/532-0500 | silveradoresort.com

RUTHERFORD/YOUNTVILLE WINERIES

1 | CLOS DU VAL

French-born Bernard Portet—winemaker here since the beginning, in 1972—makes lean and complex Cabs from Stags Leap District fruit, as well as less serious (and more affordable) wines. His first vintage was chosen for the original Judgment of Paris showdown between Bordeaux and California Cabs in 1976, and it won overall in a rematch 10 years later. Spring for the reserve tasting at the laid-back bar.

5330 Silverado Trail, Napa | 800/993-9463 | closduval.com

2 | CHIMNEY ROCK WINERY

Striking in a 17th-century Cape Dutch sort of way, Chimney Rock produces a notable Fumé Blanc, a great rosé of Cab Franc, and elegant Cabernets—numerous banners bearing 90-plus Parker scores hang from the ceiling.

5350 Silverado Trail, Napa | 800/257-2641 | chimneyrock.com

3 | STAG'S LEAP WINE CELLARS

No bells and whistles, but the tasting room hugs the fermenting tanks, and you get a chance to try today's version of the famous Cask 23 that bested Bordeaux in 1976.

5766 Silverado Trail, Napa | 707/261-6441 | cask23.com

4 | SILVERADO VINEYARDS

This huge, Disney family–owned stone and stucco winery presides over the central hills. Grand views from the tasting room are the draw at this most California-feeling place.

6121 Silverado Trail, Napa | 707/257-1770 | silveradovineyards.com

5 | ROBERT SINSKEY VINEYARDS

A tall central redwood nave grows out of low stone walls surrounded by a kitchen garden—an earth cathedral of sorts. And Robert Sinskey takes careful care of the earth, with biodynamic farming methods. The product: beautifully crafted Pinot Noirs and crisp, aromatic whites like the Abraxis blend of Alsatian grapes. Taste in the nave, with nibbles at hand and maybe a cooking class working in the tiny teaching kitchen.

6320 Silverado Trail, Napa | 800/869-2030 | robertsinskey.com

6 | CLIFF LEDE VINEYARDS

The deceptively simple Craftsman tasting room gives way to a small art gallery and a courtyard that keeps its serenity in the busiest Napa seasons. Cliff Lede Cabernet is one of Napa's latest greats. (The vineyard's nearby Poetry Inn is a splurge that's worth it.)

1473 Yountville Cross Road, Yountville | 800/428-2259 | cliffledevineyards.com

Continues page 20 >

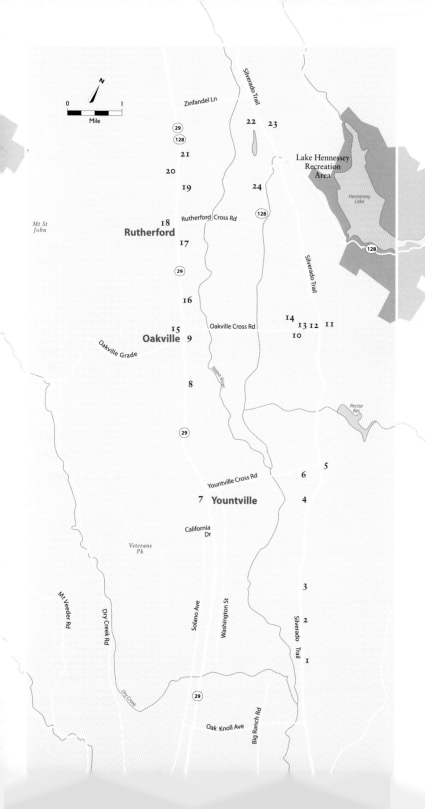

7 | DOMAINE CHANDON

Surrounded by gardens, ponds, and art, Domaine Chandon is a beautiful introduction to the valley and to sparkling-wine making. Take a look at riddling and blending techniques before you order some appetizers in the salon and find out how well sparkling wine pairs with food. Or treat yourself to a special meal with bubbles at étoile, Chandon's dressed-up restaurant.

1 California Drive, Yountville | 707/944-2280 | chandon.com

8 | CARDINALE

Part of the growing Kendall-Jackson empire now, this imposing stone winery encompasses a knoll in the center of the valley, offering world-class views as well as a chance to taste the Robert Parker-praised red blend by the same name. A second brand is poured here, Atalon, with multiple Merlots that give you a chance to compare vineyards on Howell and Veeder mountains.

7600 St. Helena Highway, Oakville | 800/588-0279 | cardinale.com

9 | NAPA WINE CO.

Several dozen wineries—from Lamborn Family Vineyards, whose grapes grow on Howell Mountain, to Fife, which has vineyards in Napa and Mendocino's Redwood Valley—sell their wines at this Oakville tasting room.

40 St. Helena Highway, Oakville | 800/848-9630 (call for appointment) | napawineco.com

10 | SILVER OAK CELLARS

Highly sought after, Silver Oaks' Napa Cab might have launched the cult-wine phenomenon. A landmark old wood tower marks the Napa estate (they have a facility in Alexander Valley too), where you can find out for yourself what all the fuss is about.

915 Oakville Cross Road, Oakville | 800/273-8809 | silveroak.com

11 | MINER FAMILY VINEYARDS

This Mediterranean villa perched above Silverado Trail offers panoramic views from its terraces and hides extensive caves in the hill behind. Excellent versions of a wide range of wines (not all from Napa grapes) are crafted here, from Viognier to a lovely dry rosé, but Miner Family's classic Oakville Cabernet is a standout.

7850 Silverado Trail, Oakville | 800/366-9463 | minerwines.com

12 | RUDD VINEYARDS & WINERY

In Napa terms a relative newcomer, Leslie Rudd (who also owns the Dean & Deluca chain) has started at the top of the class, beginning with his location among Oakville Cross Road's royalty. The beautiful stone facility has extensive gardens and underground caves—it's also producing first-class wines. Visiting here is an event: You can take a full tour, which ends with food-and-wine pairings (the work of Dean & Deluca's executive chef), or you can arrange to just taste the wines.

500 Oakville Cross Road, Oakville | 707/944-8577 (call for appointment) | ruddwines.com

13 | PLUMPJACK WINERY

Follow the Falstaff crests that zigzag you through the vineyards to this pedigreed, celebritied winery. Billionaire Gordon Getty and San Francisco politician Gavin Newsom are behind the Jack Falstaff fun here (named for Shakespeare's stout funny man, about whom Getty wrote an opera). The signature Cabernet is wonderful and daring enough to have been the first high-end red to go to market under screw caps. PlumpJack does a knockout Sauvignon Blanc and Syrah too.

620 Oakville Cross Road, Oakville | 707/945-1220 | plumpjack.com

14 | GROTH VINEYARDS & WINERY

Armed with a track record that includes having made the first California wine (a 1985 reserve Cab) to earn Robert Parker's perfect-100 score, this family winery has recently replanted all of its Oakville Cabernet Sauvignon and renovated the barrel, crush, and fermentation areas in its grand, Spanish-style facility.

750 Oakville Cross Road, Oakville | 707/754-4254 (call for appointment) | grothwines.com

15 | ROBERT MONDAVI WINERY

This hub of Napa's wine traffic might have the air of a tourist attraction, but Robert Mondavi—the man and the winery—has earned it. With a conviction that Napa wines could stand tall with any in the world, Mondavi arguably put the valley on the map. His winery (now owned by Constellation Brands) shares its architect—Cliff May—and

FAVORITES & DISCOVERIES ☆ NAPA VALLEY

STAG'S LEAP WINE CELLARS *The source of the Cabernet that for more than three decades has been giving French winemakers fits.*

PLUMPJACK WINERY *This winery has only been around since the mid-1990s but its vineyards have been in operation since the 1880s.*

SCHRAMSBERG VINEYARDS *Be sure to make an appointment to learn how sparkling wine is made, Napa style.*

CHATEAU MONTELENA *Visit this award-winning winery's ivy-draped stone castle at the far north end of the valley.*

Mission style with Sunset's headquarters. Tours here are informative if crowded. If you want to focus on high-end wine, drive across the highway to Opus One, Robert Mondavi's partnership with the Baroness Philippine de Rothschild, and pay the higher fee to taste Napa's version of a grand cru. Take your glass out on the terrace for a view to match.

7801 St. Helena Highway, Oakville | 888/766-6328 | robertmondaviwinery.com

16 | CAKEBREAD CELLARS

The only sign is on the mailbox, but the hulking, barnlike structure is hard to miss. Cakebread offers a variety of informative tours and sessions, from wine sensory education to food and wine pairing (supplied by the in-house chef). For many, its Chardonnay has become a synonym for California Chard.

8300 St. Helena Highway, Rutherford | 800/588-0298 (call for appointment) | cakebread.com

17 | ST. SUPÉRY VINEYARDS AND WINERY

The large, airy visitor center here offers as wide a range of experiences as any in the valley, from self-guided tours that include the art gallery upstairs and historic Atkinson House next door to cheese pairings and grape stomps. The focus here is on the classic Bordeaux grapes; the Sauvignon Blanc is perennially good, and the red and white blends (Élu and Virtú, respectively) led the Meritage movement.

8440 St. Helena Highway, Rutherford | 800/942-0809 | stsupery.com

18 | RUBICON ESTATE

A must-visit, if you're looking for Napa's roots. The grand Inglenook château, built by sea-captain-turned-wine-pioneer Gustave Niebaum, has watched over the valley since 1880. Movie director Francis Ford Coppola bought the estate in 1975 and has since reunited all the original vineyards. The $25 entrance fee is steep, but the tour, tasting, and museum of wine and movie making are rich.

1991 St. Helena Highway, Rutherford | 800/782-4266 | rubiconestate.com

19 | BEAULIEU VINEYARDS

The hospitable hexagonal tasting room seems modest considering the history of Napa wine masters who have worked in the historic stone winery next door. In the 1920s, Frenchman Georges de Latour bought the 1885 structure in order to produce more of the sacramental wines that were keeping his business going during Prohibition. But it was the legendary Russian-born winemaker André Tchelistcheff, brought over by Georges de Latour in 1938, who became mentor to a whole generation of vintners and changed Napa winemaking forever.

1960 St. Helena Highway, Rutherford | 800/264-6918, ext. 5235 | bvwine.com

20 | GRGICH HILLS CELLAR

One of the few rustic wineries left on the main drag. You'll find only wine and a young crowd tasting it in this friendly redwood room—no wine-gadget folderol. Mike Grgich made the Chateau Montelena Chardonnay that beat out the white Burgundies in the landmark 1976 Paris tasting, so it's no surprise he's made the grape important here.

1829 St. Helena Highway, Rutherford | 800/532-3057 | grgich.com

21 | FRANCISCAN OAKVILLE ESTATE

Now owned by the same parent company as Robert Mondavi Winery, Franciscan has one of the great tasting rooms on Highway 29—sleek and warm, with substance offered in the form of info around the room and knowing comments from the staff. Franciscan's Magnificat is one of the country's most popular Meritage (Bordeaux) blends. Mount Veeder Winery (which has the same parent company) pours here too; it's worth the extra fee to taste the reserves.

1178 Galleron Road, St. Helena | 800/529-9463 | franciscan.com

22 | QUINTESSA

There's only one wine here, and it's expensive. But it's worth making an appointment for a sit-down tasting of a couple of vintages of Quintessa, paired with cheeses, and to tour this artful, smartly designed winery. The organic-feeling stone-and-concrete facility reflects Chilean-born winemaker/co-owner Valeria Huneeus's passion for biodynamic farming and husband/partner Agustin's business savvy (he was a partner at Franciscan, and before that, grew Concha y Toro into Chile's largest winery).

1601 Silverado Trail, Rutherford | 707/967-1601 (call for appointment) | quintessa.com

23 | RUTHERFORD HILL WINERY

The vine-flanked arch of stones that is Rutherford Hill's entrance leads to great vistas of the valley from the eastern hills, a lovely picnic area under the oaks, fascinating caves, and bottles of good signature Merlot.

200 Rutherford Hill Road, Rutherford | 707/963-1871 | rutherfordhill.com

24 | FROG'S LEAP

Winemaker John Williams is way out in front of the industry, farming organically (wander through the heirloom orchard) and using solar power for his entire winery, which is also heated and cooled geothermally. The result is a refreshing reconnection with the land. The new tasting room is LEED-certified, which means it was built with highly renewable, low-impact materials. It's all very progressive but still feels like a farm—feel free to skip stones on the frog pond.

8815 Conn Creek Road, Rutherford | 800/959-4704 | frogsleap.com

THINGS TO DO

NAPA VALLEY BIKE TOURS

Napa Valley's backroads (and even the Silverado Trail) are ideal for cycling: quiet, mostly flat, beautiful. Napa Valley Bike Tours offers both rentals and guided tours.

6488 Washington Street, Yountville | **800/707-2453** | **napavalleybiketours.com**

NAPA VALLEY MUSEUM

On a hillside above Yountville, this airy museum showcases art upstairs and wine downstairs. Check out its first-rate exhibit, *California Wine: The Science of an Art*.

55 President's Circle, Yountville | **707-944-0500** | **napavalleymuseum.org**

PICNIC

Given the abundance of good food, wine, and quiet sylvan spots, the Napa Valley may just be the picnic capital of the world. Good places to acquire supplies are **Oakville Grocery** (7856 St. Helena Highway, Oakville; 707/944-8802; oakvillegrocery.com) and **Dean & DeLuca** (page 31). Good parks include **Bale Grist Mill State Historic Park** and **Bothe Napa Valley State Park** (page 30).

WHERE TO EAT

BOUCHON

The French Laundry's casual cousin. Thomas Keller oversees this stylish French cafe with the exacting standards you'd expect. Mussels and frites are all you need here, but much more seafood is available, plus quiche and other classics.

6534 Washington Street, Yountville | **707/944-8037** | **frenchlaundry.com**

BISTRO JEANTY

Hearty pâtés, French onion soup, tongue salad, steak frites—all the greatest hits of an authentic French bistro are here. And because French-born Philippe Jeanty (formerly of Domaine Chandon) is cooking, they're delicious.

6510 Washington Street, Yountville | **707/944-0103** | **bistrojeanty.com**

REDD

Richard Reddington brings an air of Napa Valley royalty to his first namesake restaurant, what with his romance with Robert Mondavi's granddaughter and history as chef at Auberge du Soleil. He offers four-, six-, and nine-course tasting menus, with influences from the Mediterranean, Asia, and Mexico.

6480 Washington Street, Yountville | **707/944-2222** | **reddnapavalley.com**

THE FRENCH LAUNDRY

What more is there to say about a street-corner cottage turned into one of the best restaurants in the country? Plan to make reservations two months ahead and to pay more than you've ever paid for dinner. This is grand cooking.

6640 Washington Street, Yountville | 707/944-2380 | frenchlaundry.com

PLACES TO STAY

AUBERGE DU SOLEIL

Everyone's favorite Napa Valley splurge: Set on an olive-covered hillside, the resort has large rooms, stunning views, and a notable restaurant. 50 rooms from $525.

180 Rutherford Hill Road, Rutherford | 800/348-5406 | aubergedusoleil.com

LAVENDER

There are indeed ample lavender gardens here, but also charming country French guest rooms. 8 rooms from $225.

2020 Webber Street, Yountville | 800/522-4140 | lavendernapa.com

MAISON FLEURIE

The pool is welcome after a warm day of wine tasting. 13 rooms from $125.

6529 Yount Street, Yountville | 800/788-0369 | foursisters.com

NAPA VALLEY LODGE

Tuscan-style lodge at the north end of Yountville. 55 rooms from $279.

2230 Madison Street, Yountville | 707/944-2468 | woodsidehotels.com

RANCHO CAYMUS INN

Appealing inn is rich in old California atmosphere—each room is named for some famous or infamous figure from Napa Valley history. 26 rooms from $155.

1140 Rutherford Road, Rutherford | 707/963-1777 | ranchocaymus.com

VILLAGIO INN & SPA

Posh Italian-style resort that lavishes amenities on guests. 112 rooms from $230.

6481 Washington Street, Yountville | 800/351-1133 | villagio.com

VINTAGE INN

Lovely, Provence-influenced inn. 80 rooms from $230.

6541 Washington Street, Yountville | 707/944-1112 | vintageinn.com

ST. HELENA & CALISTOGA WINERIES

1 | KULETO ESTATE

Tucked in the hills east of St. Helena on former cattle-ranch land, well-known restaurant designer Pat Kuleto's stone winery is a 750-acre world unto itself. It's a serious detour off Silverado Trail, but the rewards include an amazing setting and rustic yet refined wines.

2470 Sage Canyon Road, St. Helena | 707/963-9750 (call for appointment) | kuletoestate.com

2 | JOSEPH PHELPS VINEYARDS

After making an appointment to visit Kuleto, make a second appointment to visit Joesph Phelps. One of Napa's earliest—and still most important—Bordeaux blends (Insignia) lurks in this cavernous redwood winery at the end of a beautiful winding drive through tucked-away vineyards. Joseph Phelps's Rhône blend, Le Mistral, is another good reason to come here.

200 Taplin Road, St. Helena | 707/963-2745 (call for appointment) | jpvwines.com

3 | WHITEHALL LANE WINERY

This winery is coming on strong for its quality. The concrete-floor tasting room of this modern, color-block structure has a friendly vibe—try Whitehall's beautifully structured Cabs, one of which (the reserve) was the first wine in this country to be bottled under the radical new glass stopper called Vino-Seal. Check it out.

1563 St. Helena Highway, St. Helena | 800/963-9454, ext. 19 | whitehalllane.com

4 | CORISON WINERY

Cathy Corison makes two very special Cabernets in her graceful barn of a winery. One is made from grapes grown in the surrounding Kronos Vineyard, which is one of the oldest Cab vineyards in the valley. The tasting "room" is right in the winery's working space, making a visit to Corison a full-circle experience.

987 St. Helena Highway, St. Helena | 707/963-0826 (call for appointment) | corison.com

5 | HEITZ CELLARS

Lovely little lodgelike tasting room, where you can try the Martha's Vineyard Cab made famous by the late, larger-than-life winemaker Joe Heitz, who worked under the legendary André Tchelistcheff at Beaulieu Vineyards during the middle of the last century. Joe's son David makes the wine now.

436 St. Helena Highway South, St. Helena | 707/963-3542 | heitzcellar.com

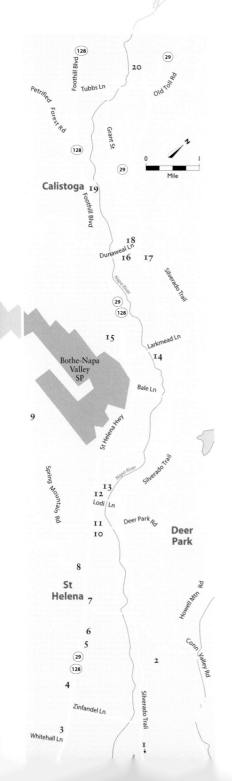

6 | LOUIS M. MARTINI WINERY

This stone monolith of a winery might be owned by the Gallo family now, but the legacy launched by Louis Martini in 1933 lives on. The tasting room has been remodeled, and the wines keep getting better under the direction of winemaker-grandson Michael Martini.

254 South St. Helena Highway, St. Helena | 800/321-9463 | louismartini.com

7 | MERRYVALE VINEYARDS

Groundbreaking from the start as the valley's first post-Prohibition winery, Merryvale is still lively, with great weekend-morning tasting seminars that get you into the historic cask room. Combine a visit to Merryvale Vineyards with lunch or dinner at Tra Vigne next door.

1000 Main Street, St. Helena | 707/963-7777 | merryvale.com

8 | BERINGER VINEYARDS

The oldest continually operating winery in the valley, and a St. Helena landmark, Beringer offers a whole menu of tours, some focused on the winery's past (its Rhine House and wine caves are synonymous with Napa history), others devoted to the juice in the bottles. There are even two tasting rooms. You're inundated with Chardonnays here, but try a Howell Mountain and Private Reserve Cab if you can.

2000 Main Street, St. Helena | 707/963-7115 | beringer.com

9 | SMITH MADRONE VINEYARDS & WINERY

The dry Riesling alone is worth the short drive through the redwoods up Spring Mountain just west of St. Helena to Stuart and Charles Smith's place. But you might get a folding picnic chair to sit on, and Stuart's likely to use his Swiss Army knife to open the wine.

**4022 Spring Mountain Road, St. Helena |
707/963-2283 (call for appointment) | smithmadrone.com**

10 | CHARLES KRUG

Long owned by the Peter Mondavi family, this winery had to take a back seat on the fame train when brother Robert broke away and founded his eponymous house. Still, Charles Krug is the oldest winery in the Napa Valley (established in 1861), and no trip to Napa would be complete without a stop at the historic (if a little tired) structure.

2800 Main Street, St. Helena | 800/682-5784 | charleskrug.com

11 | MARKHAM VINEYARDS

Markham is an old winery with young taste. The beautiful stone facility in its center dates to 1879, but the visitor area doubles as a modern art gallery and the courtyard frequently has live music.

**2812 St. Helena Highway North, St. Helena | 707/963-5292 |
markhamvineyards.com**

12 | A DOZEN VINTNERS

This collective specializes in boutique wines made from grapes grown on Spring, Diamond, and Howell mountains.

3000 St. Helena Highway, St. Helena | 707/967-0666 | adozenvintners.com

13 | DUCKHORN VINEYARDS

Check in at the front desk, restaurant style, for sit-down tastings in this gracious, porched tasting center. Duckhorn wines have a great following across the country. The company's newer, "second-label" tasting room, Paraduxx, farther south on Silverado Trail, is even more fun: an old vineyard farmhouse turned modern, with sleek bar tables and lounge chairs on a great back porch overlooking an area with picnic tables.

**1000 Lodi Lane, St. Helena | 888/354-8885 (call for appointment) |
duckhorn.com**

14 | FRANK FAMILY VINEYARDS

Housed in the historic 1884 Larkmead Winery, Frank Family Vineyards produces several sparkling wines, a fruity Sangiovese, and a rich Cabernet Sauvignon, the latter from grapes grown entirely on Winston Hill in the Rutherford appellation.

1091 Larkmead Lane, Calistoga | 800/574-9463 | frankfamilyvineyards.com

15 | SCHRAMSBERG VINEYARDS

History was made here in 1965, when Jack and Jamie Davies bought the already-historic winery (second-oldest in the valley, founded by German immigrants Jacob and Annie Schram in 1862) and were the first in the country to make sparkling wine. The tour gives you a look at a mind-boggling 2 million bottles of bubbles in 2 miles of underground caves dug out at the turn of the last century, plus interesting info about hand riddling, dosage, and other sparkling wine–making techniques.

1400 Schramsberg Road, Calistoga | 800/877-3623 (call for appointment) | schramsberg.com

16 | STERLING VINEYARDS

It's a time-consuming undertaking to visit one of the most popular stops in the valley, but the tram ride up to this gleaming white, Greek-meets-Mission-style monolith is one of the most dramatic ways to view the valley. Sterling has put its signature on Merlot; there are interesting vineyard comparisons to be had here.

1111 Dunaweal Lane, Calistoga | 800/726-6136 | sterlingvineyards.com

17 | CUVAISON ESTATE WINES

A simple, hospitable getaway from Napa's core traffic, with yummy wines from Carneros and Mt. Veeder. The oak trees make a great picnic canopy.

4550 Silverado Trail North, Calistoga | 707/942-6266 | cuvaison.com

18 | CLOS PEGASE

This striking "temple to wine and art," designed by architect Michael Graves, houses an art collection but is itself the real work of art worth stopping for. The Mitsuko's Vineyard wines are special—founder Jan Shrem's wife is the namesake.

1060 Dunaweal Lane, Calistoga | 707/942-4981 | clospegase.com

19 | THE WINE GARAGE

This warehouse-style retail shop and tasting room sits next to a 1940s filling station. Of the 200-some wines and 3,000-plus bottles on hand, most are from California and all are under $25—refreshing in this pricey valley.

1020 Foothill Boulevard, Calistoga | 707/942-5332 | winegarage.net

20 | CHATEAU MONTELENA

One of the most serene spots in the valley. Wander around spring-fed Jade Lake and taste in the ivy-draped 1880s stone castle seemingly built from the mountain it leans against. Montelena's Chardonnay is historic too—its 1973 version bested all the white Burgundies in the Judgment of Paris tasting of 1976.

1429 Tubbs Lane, Calistoga | 707/942-5105 | montelena.com

THINGS TO DO

BALE GRIST MILL STATE HISTORIC PARK

Napa wasn't always all about wine: This working flour mill dates from 1846. On weekends, rangers still grind grain here.

3369 St. Helena Highway North, St. Helena | **707/942-4575**

BOTHE NAPA VALLEY STATE PARK

A lovely place for a wine country picnic, plus a swimming pool and 50 camp sites. One of the park trails leads 1.2 miles to Bale Grist Mill State Historic Park (see above).

3801 St. Helena Highway North, St. Helena | **707/942-4575**

CULINARY INSTITUTE OF AMERICA AT GREYSTONE

Gray stones indeed: The California branch of the famed New York–based culinary institute occupies a glorious Romanesque building that was once the largest stone winery in the world. Aspiring chefs and sommeliers vie to attend here. Visitors can buy cookware and foodstuffs at Spice Islands Marketplace, stroll the edible gardens, and dine simply at De Baun Cafe or more elaborately at the institute's restaurant, Wine Spectator's Greystone.

2555 Main Street, St. Helena | **707/967-1010 (restaurant reservations)** | **ciachef.edu**

DOWNTOWN ST. HELENA

Our Town meets *Beverly Hills 90210* along St. Helena's Main Street, where sensible stores catering to locals mix with chic boutiques and galleries catering to well-heeled visitors. At Crane Park, a few blocks southwest, the Friday morning farmer's market is considered one of the best in the valley.

DR. WILKINSON'S HOT SPRINGS RESORT

Go for "the Works," a traditional mud bath with facial mask, aromatic mineral whirlpool bath, steam room, and blanket wrap. There are also 42 motel units from $109, as well as cottages and bungalows.

1507 Lincoln Avenue, Calistoga | **707/942-4102** | **drwilkinson.com**

INDIAN SPRINGS SPA

Calistoga pioneer Sam Brannan laid the tracks for the Napa Wine Train in 1864 to bring guests from Napa and points beyond to this resort, where mud baths feature volcanic ash and hot mineral water. You can also stay in one of 17 bungalows that start at $285.

1712 Lincoln Avenue, Calistoga | **707/942-4913** | **indianspringscalistoga.com**

ROBERT LOUIS STEVENSON STATE PARK

Treasure Island author Stevenson honeymooned (in a bunkhouse) here in 1880. It's still wild and lovely: The 10-mile (round-trip) hike up and down Mt. St. Helena offers some of the best views in Northern California.

3801 St. Helena Highway, Calistoga | **707/942-4575**

ST. HELENA CYCLERY

Rent a road bike or a hybrid, and get expert advice on the valley's best routes.

1156 Main Street, Helena | **707/963-7736** | **sthelenacyclery.com**

PLACES TO EAT

CINDY'S BACKSTREET KITCHEN

Cindy is, of course, wine country restaurateur Cindy Pawlcyn. Her "kitchen" occupies a charming two-story house in downtown St. Helena. The atmosphere is that of a welcoming country inn somewhere in the south; the menu is California comfort foods (meat loaf, tamales) with a twist. Fine desserts.

1327 Railroad Avenue, St. Helena | **707/963-1200** | **cindysbackstreetkitchen.com**

DEAN & DELUCA

Don't tell New Yorkers, but the St. Helena branch of Manhattan's foodie mainstay may be even more alluring to palates (and wallets) than the SoHo original.

607 South St. Helena Highway, St. Helena | **707/967-9980** | **deandeluca.com**

GO FISH

Busy Cindy Pawlcyn has filled the longtime Napa Valley need for a good seafood restaurant. The sushi bar, presided over by master Ken Tominaga, is destination enough for many, but the menu in the dining room highlights some of Pawlcyn's favorite flavors from the American south, Latin America, and Asia. Choose from the menu or mix and match from the "Fish your way" part of the list.

641 Main Street, St. Helena | **707/963-0700** | **gofishrestaurant.net**

MARTINI HOUSE

Chef Todd Humphries and Pat Kuleto teamed up to turn this historic, side-street St. Helena house into the best sort of wine-country restaurant. Humphries favors foraged and organic ingredients—game, wild mushrooms, and the like. Grilled tenderloin comes with crushed summer truffles, oregano, and wine-stewed onions.

1245 Spring Street, St. Helena | **707/963-2233** | **martinihouse.com**

PRESS

The best ingredients to be had are cooked simply at this warm, stylish steakhouse, with the most inviting bar in town. The New York strip and rib-eye are standouts; the roast chicken is carved tableside, and the kitchen has a deft hand with seasonal sides like ratatouille. Luckily, the garlic and potato cake is always in season. The goal of the wine list is impressive: to include a bottle from every winery in Napa Valley. It comes close—and gives you nuggets about each winemaker or owner besides.

587 St. Helena Highway South, St. Helena | 707/967-0550 | presssthelena.com

TAYLOR'S AUTOMATIC REFRESHER

Come all the way to Napa Valley for a burger and a shake? Yes, when it's the Wisconsin sourdough burger and a black-and-white shake at this valley institution. There are more contemporary offerings (ahi burgers, salads) for those who eschew the classics.

933 Main Street, St. Helena | 707/963-3486 | taylorsrefresher.com

TERRA

Some of the most creative cooking in St. Helena is found in a restored 19th-century stone building a block off Main Street. Chef Hiro Sone combines California cuisine with native Japanese ingredients in dishes like the signature sake-marinated Alaskan black cod and shrimp dumplings in shiso broth.

1345 Railroad Avenue, St. Helena | 707/963-8931 | terrarestaurant.com

WAPPO BAR & BISTRO

Multiethnic before fusion was all the rage, Wappo's menu spans the globe, from a chiles relleno appetizer—poblanos stuffed with creamy rice and currants in a walnut-pomegranate sauce—to Thai green curry halibut, tandoori chicken, cassoulet, and osso buco. The patio, with its twisted grapevines and fountain, is the place to be.

1226 Washington Street, Calistoga | 707/942-4712 | wappobar.com

WHERE TO STAY

BRANNAN COTTAGE INN

History buffs take note: This lovely little inn occupies the oldest building in Calistoga, the sole survivor of the 14 cottages town founder Sam Brannan built for his hot springs resort. 6 rooms from $145.

109 Wappo Avenue, Calistoga | 707/942-4200 | brannancottageinn.com

CALISTOGA RANCH

Sibling to Auberge du Soleil, this resort rests in a 157-acre canyon in the mountains east of Calistoga. Secluded and luxurious, it has its own spa along with 4 miles of hiking trails. 46 lodges from $575.

580 Lommel Road, Calistoga | **800/942-4220** | **calistogaranch.com**

COTTAGE GROVE INN

A collection of new but traditionally styled Craftsman cottages, each with its own theme—e.g., "Provence," "Nautical." 16 cottages from $235.

1711 Lincoln Avenue, Calistoga | **800/799-2284** | **cottagegrove.com**

EL BONITA MOTEL

For years, this classic motel with the sleek neon sign was a cherished Napa Valley secret. Now word is out, which means you'll need to book in advance. But the reasonable rates and the great retro road trip vibes remain. 42 rooms from $90.

195 Main Street, St. Helena | **707/963-3216** | **elbonita.com**

HOTEL ST. HELENA

Reasonable rates and a convenient location in downtown St. Helena make this historic hotel a good option. 18 rooms (14 with private bath) from $125.

1309 Main Street, St. Helena | **707/963-4388** | **hotelsthelena.com**

MEADOWOOD RESORT

One of the most elegant retreats in Northern California. Meadowood's green lawns (croquet is big here) and New England–style cottages whisper old money, although in fact the resort is only 40 years old. 85 rooms and cottages from $500.

900 Meadowood Lane, St. Helena | **800/458-8080** | **meadowood.com**

MOUNT VIEW HOTEL

A handsomely restored 1917 hotel. 32 rooms from $169.

1457 Lincoln Avenue, Calistoga | **707/942-6877** | **mountviewhotel.com**

SILVER ROSE INN

Two inns, actually: the Inn on the Knoll and the Inn on the Vineyard—the latter named for the 10 acres of vines on the property. 20 rooms from $165.

351 Rosedale Road, Calistoga | **800/995-9381** | **silverrose.com**

THE INN AT SOUTHBRIDGE

Stylish, very luxurious inn just south of downtown St. Helena. 21 rooms from $255.

1020 Main Street, St. Helena | **800/520-6800** | **innatsouthbridge.com**

OF ALL CALIFORNIA'S WINE REGIONS, Sonoma may be the easiest
to fall in love with, if falling in love with a place means visiting and not
wanting to leave. In part, Sonoma has the advantage of sheer size. At more
than 1,500 square miles, it's as big as Rhode Island, and those square
miles manage to encompass all the best things about the entire state of
California. For a classically beautiful valley, the Sonoma Valley—a.k.a.
the Valley of the Moon—can't be bettered. For old California–tinged
history, stroll Sonoma Plaza and visit Mission San Francisco de Solano.
For really big trees, hike Armstrong Redwoods State Reserve. For a
rugged coastline, head a few miles west to Jenner.

That roster of pleasures doesn't even include what you came for: the
county's dozen or so appellations and 200-some-odd wineries. It's only
about half as many wine producers as there are in Napa Valley, Sonoma's
soft-rival sibling to the east. And while it's impossible not to attempt
comparisons between the two preeminent wine regions in the state, the
most that can be said is that Sonoma County takes great pleasure in not
being Napa. And that says much about the experience you'll have here.

If anything, Sonoma's wine history reaches even further back than
Napa's (although they share some roots, so to speak). The first grapevines
were planted at Mission San Francisco de Solano in 1824, and that vineyard was where George Yount got his vines to plant over in the Napa
Valley a few years later. In time, General Mariano Vallejo came to own
the mission holdings here, built up the town of Sonoma, and planted his
own vineyard. The first vintage produced from grapes grown on Jacob
Gundlach's Rhinefarm was poured in 1861—you drive through the vineyard to reach Gundlach Bundschu to this day. By the late 1800s, there

were in the neighborhood of 120 wineries in the county, including Korbel and Simi; Sebastiani came on the scene just after the turn of the century.

If Napa was the destination for the wealthy seeking a showcase retreat, Sonoma was home to winemaking religious cults, communes, and co-ops more interested in isolation, including the Italian Swiss Colony in Asti. And while the old wine houses have grown into major operations now (some of the largest are here: Clos du Bois, Kendall-Jackson, Gallo), it's still a place where ambitious winemakers—Rick Hutchinson of Amphora in Dry Creek Valley; Nick and Andy Peay and Vanessa Wong of Peay Vineyards on the coast—have a prayer of a chance of getting a foothold in the business. The result is a range of wine personalities.

But beyond the eclectic nature of Sonoma winemakers, it's the wildly disparate geography that makes the region impossible to summarize. The county sprawls through warm valleys shielded from any Pacific influence and cool ones defined by ocean wind and fog, over inland mountains cooled by altitude and coastal hills that poke above the fog for warmth. It is largely temperature that distinguishes Sonoma County's AVAs from one another, and determines the grapes that have become their various signature wines.

On the eastern side, the cooling breezes off San Pablo Bay make the Carneros region (which Sonoma shares with Napa) a great place for Pinot Noir and Chardonnay—both still and bubbly versions, from such places as Domaine Carneros and Gloria Ferrer. The cooling effect peters out as you get into Sonoma Valley proper, so warmer-weather grapes thrive: Sauvignon Blanc, Cabernet, Zinfandel, Syrah. Farther north, in toasty Knights and Alexander valleys, soft Cabs and Merlots reign; go no further than to Jordan Vineyards to find out why. To the west, planting decisions are based on where you are in relation to the Petaluma Gap, which lets the Russian River out to the sea and sends mighty cool air in the other direction. The Russian River Valley is a remote and beautiful home for Pinot Noir and Chardonnay—its Green Valley appellation, with the likes of Iron Horse and Marimar Torres, the coolest of all. But follow the Russian River north into Dry Creek Valley and Zin is the subject. The very cold outer reaches of the Sonoma Coast appellation are

Continues page 37 >

SUGGESTED ROUTES

☆ **SONOMA TO KENWOOD** *Follow Highway 12 north from Sonoma to Kenwood, return via Warm Springs Road and Arnold Drive*

☆ **HEALDSBURG TO MONTE RIO** *Go south on Westside Road to River Road*

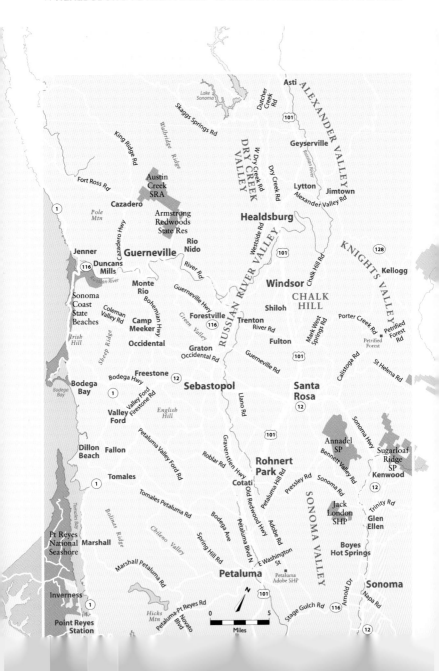

becoming awfully interesting places for Pinot, Chardonnay, and Syrah; unfortunately, you can't visit many of the wineries out there yet.

Sonoma County's size, diversity, and large number of wineries mean that it works as a destination for a weekend or even longer. Choose your base of operations depending on the kinds of wines you want to explore (i.e., cooler- or warmer-weather varietals); settle in near the appellations you most want to tour. The town of Sonoma has its famous plaza and easy access to the wineries of Sonoma Valley and Carneros. To the north, Healdsburg is convenient for touring the Alexander Valley, Dry Creek, and Russian River wine regions. It's also become one of Northern California's capitals of chic. Explore its downtown, noting the mix of homespun stores and world-class restaurants and hotels, and you find yourself thinking: If Norman Rockwell and Miuccia Prada joined forces to design their ideal small town, it would probably be something like this. Santa Rosa, the county seat, is pretty much central to everything; Guerneville, on the Russian River, is good if you want to mix wine touring with camping, canoeing, and other outdoor activities.

With all this going for it, it's probably no coincidence that Sonoma County inspired three writers whose works evoked the California dream at its most pleasurable and potent. America's greatest writer on food, M.F.K. Fisher, had her loyalties to the Napa Valley—she lived in St. Helena for decades. Still, in the latter part of her life she opted to live and write in Sonoma County's tiny Glen Ellen. Not too far away are the stomping grounds of another symbol of American joie de vivre: *Peanuts'* Snoopy, whose creator, Charles Schulz, called Santa Rosa home. If the leap from exuberant beagle to peerless Cabernet seems a long one, don't forget— Snoopy's capacious doghouse contained its own wine cellar.

Finally, there's Sonoma County's most famous writer, dashing Jack London, memorialized now in the Glen Ellen state park that bears his name. His short novel *Valley of the Moon* told of a young couple's journey up and down the length of California, seeking a place to call home. "What we want," they said, "is a valley of the moon, with not too much work and all the fun we want. And we'll just keep on looking until we find it." As the name of the novel hints, they found that perfect place in Sonoma County. Chances are you will too.

SONOMA VALLEY WINERIES

I | GLORIA FERRER CHAMPAGNE CAVES

Like a Spanish monastery, Gloria Ferrer guards lower Sonoma and offers great vistas over it. Order the sparkling-wine tasting of your choice at the counter, than take a table on the terrace and munch nibbles with your bubbles. The sparklers at this Spanish-owned house are consistently good, and the still Pinot Noirs greatly interesting; compare the versions from Gravel Knob and Rust Rock Terrace.

23555 Carneros Highway, Sonoma | 707/933-1917 | gloriaferrer.com

2 | ROBLEDO FAMILY WINERY

This was the first winery in the state owned by a former Mexican migrant worker. The Robledos now own 1,800 acres of vineyards too, and their own wines can be sampled in a cozy tasting room. All the Robledo children work in the business; a son-in-law is the winemaker, and his wines commemorating family members are worth seeking out.

21901 Bonness Road, Sonoma | 707/939-6903 | robledofamilywinery.com

3 | GUNDLACH BUNDSCHU WINERY

One of the oldest family wineries in California (and heaviest on consonants in the name), Gundlach Bundschu makes the most of its grand setting, with picnic tables under an arbor, bike trails, a wine cave (tours on the hour), and an old-feeling stone tasting room. The traditional varieties have classic profiles, with good acidity to keep them alive, but try the Tempranillo from the Rhinefarm vineyard you drove through to get here; it's Spain's main red grape, and GB is one of the few wineries making it in CA.

2000 Denmark Street, Sonoma | 707/939-3015 | gunbun.com

4 | SEBASTIANI VINEYARDS & WINERY

The huge parking lot might have a "bus drop-off" sign, and the host behind the register in the hospitality center might inform you that the shop you have to navigate to get to the tasting bar offers 5,000 tabletop items, but Sebastiani breathes history. A visit here gets you close to the stones and wood casks of more than a century's worth of California winemaking. There are trolley tours too.

389 Fourth Street East, Sonoma | 707/933-3230 | sebastiani.com

5 | RAVENSWOOD WINERY

One of the three famous Rs of Zinfandel—Ridge and Rosenblum being the other two—this winery produces prodigious amounts of Zin. Now owned by Constellation Brands, Ravenswood is still run by founder Joel Peterson and keeps on trucking with its "No Wimpy Wines" mantra. You can find its baseline Vintners Blend in every supermarket in the land, so come here to try the fascinating single-vineyard Zinfandels.

18701 Gehricke Road, Sonoma | 707/933-2332 | ravenswood-wine.com

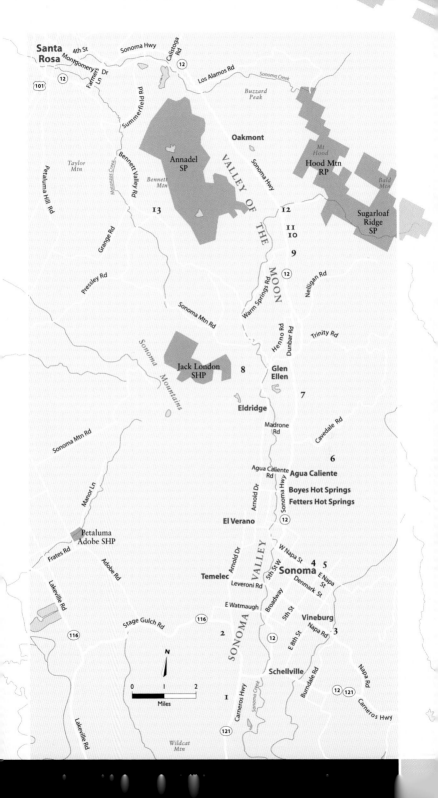

6 | MOON MOUNTAIN VINEYARD

Mountain wine is all the rage these days, but few wineries match the elevation of Moon Mountain, tucked almost 2,000 feet high up on the Sonoma side of the Mayacamas. The views are exhilarating, the steep vineyards are organic, and the 15,000-cubic-meter cave bored into pure volcanic rock is as authentic-looking as any in California.

1700 Moon Mountain Drive, Sonoma | 707/996-5870 (call for appointment) | moonmountainvineyard.com

7 | ARROWOOD VINEYARDS & WINERY

For better or for worse, depending on your taste, Dick Arrowood is partially responsible for California's quintessential big, buttery, oaky Chardonnay style. His winemaking has continued to evolve, and even though Arrowood is corporate-owned now, Dick is still involved, and still a leader in Sonoma winemaking.

14347 Sonoma Highway, Glen Ellen | 800/938-5170 | arrowoodwinery.com

8 | BENZIGER FAMILY WINERY

Take a tractor-tram tour up through the vineyards for a close-up look at biodynamic farming. Then wander through the well-signed antique equipment on the beautiful grounds; taste at the regular, reserve, or club bar.

1883 London Ranch Road, Glen Ellen | 888/490-2739 | benziger.com

9 | KUNDE ESTATE WINERY & VINEYARDS

A huge stone version of a Craftsman-style house, Kunde offers views of tanks and the bottling line from the tasting room, a great patio by the pond and fountain, cave tours, and an always-refreshing Sauvignon Blanc.

9825 Sonoma Highway, Kenwood | 707/833-5501 | kunde.com

10 | MAYO FAMILY WINERY RESERVE TASTING ROOM

The Mayo family has confused things, with three separate tasting rooms (one right on the square in Sonoma), but this one is unique in chef William Oliver's full menu of wine-and-food pairings. The Mayos produce a hefty lineup of unmanipulated, unfiltered, single-vineyard bottlings (as many as 25).

9200 Sonoma Highway, Kenwood | 707/833-5504 | mayofamilywinery.com

11 | CHATEAU ST. JEAN

Every bit the château, St. Jean is built for crowds—goods-filled tasting room, deli case with tasty cheeses and pâtés, and wonderful places to consume them. The winery's reputation rests on whites (its Sauvignon Blanc is a great favorite), but its best reds, like the Cinq Cépages blend, deserve attention.

8555 Sonoma Highway, Kenwood | 707/833-4134 | chateaustjean.com

I 2 | LANDMARK VINEYARDS

Downright homelike compared to neighboring St. Jean, the stucco Landmark, complete with bocce court, is a welcoming place to try a few choice wines—the rich but focused Overlook Chardonnay, elegant Kastania Pinot Noir, and juicy Steel Plow Syrah.

101 Adobe Canyon Road, Kenwood | **707/833-0053** | **landmarkwine.com**

I 3 | MATANZAS CREEK WINERY

Bennett Valley Road runs through one of the county's newest AVAs to Matanzas Creek, whose remarkable lavender gardens have been turned into products for its tasting-room shelves. The only downside is a mysterious lavender aroma in every wine. But take a glass of the especially aromatic Sauvignon Blanc outside to the terrace, at canopy level in the oak trees, and enjoy French winemaker Francois Cordesse's handiwork.

6097 Bennett Valley Road, Santa Rosa | **800/590-6464** | **matanzascreek.com**

SPOTLIGHT AGOSTON HARASZTHY

*High on a hill above Sonoma Valley is a memorial to the founding father of California winemaking. There are other claimants, but Agoston Haraszthy earns points for the sheer drama of his life. And death. ☆ Born in Hungary in 1812, Haraszthy arrived in the state during the Gold Rush. In the 1850s, California wines were syrupy products produced from Mission grapes. Haraszthy knew the state could do better. He bought a dormant vineyard, dubbed it Buena Vista, and built a house inspired by the villas of Pompeii. In 1861 he spent months in Europe, gathering vines to ship home, among them Cabernet Sauvignon and other varieties that anchor California's wine industry today. ☆ His showy success made his fall all the more brutal. After losing Buena Vista to unscrupulous partners, he launched a new project: a sugar plantation in Nicaragua. And there, in 1869, he vanished into an alligator-infested river. ☆ Today Haraszthy's legacy endures. Outside the tasting room of **Buena Vista** (18000 Old Winery Road, Sonoma; 800/926-1266; buenavistacarneros.com) is a monument to Haraszthy. Nearby, **Bartholomew Park Winery** (1000 Vineyard Lane, Sonoma; 707/935-9511; bartholomewparkwinery.com) has a museum devoted to his career. Down the hill is a replica of the villa. Trails run into the vineyards and a picnic area offers sweeping views of the valley, a good place to toast wine, drama, and life.*

THINGS TO DO

ANNADEL STATE PARK

Highlights of this 5,000-acre state park a few minutes east of Santa Rosa are stands of California oaks and brilliant displays of spring wildflowers.

6201 Channel Drive, Santa Rosa | 707/539-3911 | parks.ca.gov

CHARLES M. SCHULZ MUSEUM AND RESEARCH CENTER

A must-stop for anyone who grew up reading *Peanuts,* this airy museum is big enough to house Snoopy, Linus, Charlie Brown, and the other characters indelibly inked by Schulz, who for decades called Sonoma County home.

**2301 Hardies Lane, Santa Rosa | 707/579-4452 |
schulzmuseum.org**

CORNERSTONE GARDENS

At this unique and beautiful spot on the road into Sonoma, you're invited to explore 20 cutting-edge gardens designed by noted landscape architects. Open late March through early December.

**23570 Highway 121, Sonoma | 707/933-3010 |
cornerstonegardens.com**

JACK LONDON STATE HISTORIC PARK

The gifted, hard-living writer installed himself and his wife/muse Charmian on these 800 acres—which he dubbed Beauty Ranch—in 1909. Their cottage is open to visit, as is the House of Happy Walls, which holds London memorabilia preserved by Charmian after his death. The 3-mile trek up Sonoma Mountain gives you IMAX-worthy views of the whole Valley of the Moon.

2400 London Ranch Road, Glen Ellen | 707/938-5216 | parks.ca.gov

LUTHER BURBANK HOME AND GARDEN

No one took advantage of Sonoma County's rich soil and welcoming climate more assiduously than self-taught botanist Burbank, who, during his half-century career, developed the Shasta daisy, the Santa Rosa plum, and some 800 plant varieties. Today's visitors can tour his gardens and home April through October.

**Santa Rosa Avenue at Sonoma Avenue, Santa Rosa | 707/524-5445 |
lutherburbank.org**

THE OLIVE PRESS

In Jack London Village, a roadside ramble of 19th-century buildings, the Olive Press sells olive oils and olive-related items from dozens of California growers.

14301 Arnold Drive, Glen Ellen | 707/939-8900 | theolivepress.com

SAFARI WEST

The Serengeti comes to Sonoma at this 400-acre preserve filled with the animals of the African savanna: giraffe, antelope, and oryx, seen on guided tours. If you really want to live your *Out of Africa* fantasies, bunk down in one of the surprisingly elegant tent cabins. 30 cabins from $225.

3115 Porter Creek Road, Santa Rosa | 800/616-2695 |
safariwest.com

SONOMA PLAZA

The city wears its past gracefully, with some of California's most historic buildings—among them Mission San Francisco de Solano and Lachryma Montis, General Vallejo's still-Edenic estate—centered around the lawns and spreading trees of its 8-acre central plaza.

Sonoma State Historic Park, 363 Third Street West, Sonoma |
707/938-9559

SUGARLOAF RIDGE STATE PARK

This 2,700-acre park, with 25 miles of trails, preserves the headwaters of Sonoma Creek. Spring through fall, you can explore via horseback rides run by Triple Creek Horse Outfit (707/887-8700; triplecreekhorseoutfit.com).

2605 Adobe Canyon Road, Kenwood | 707/833-5712 | parks.ca.gov

WHERE TO EAT

CAFE LA HAYE

Chef/owner John McReynolds says the older he gets, the simpler his cooking becomes. The Mediterranean-flavored dishes that come out of this postage-stamp kitchen are some of the best you'll ever taste.

140 East Napa Street, Sonoma | 707/935-5994

CARNEROS BISTRO AND WINE BAR

Don't discount Carneros Bistro as a hotel restaurant (it's in The Lodge at Sonoma). The local lamb and the wild salmon are well prepared, and the wine list shows off many individual Sonoma vineyards.

1325 Broadway, Sonoma | 707/931-2042 | thelodgeatsonoma.com

DEUCE

This warm, artful restaurant gets little outside press but is a resident favorite for creative, local-ingredient cooking.

691 Broadway, Sonoma | 707/933-3823 | dine-at-deuce.com

EL DORADO KITCHEN

The cool bar and outdoor lounge area might be a hangout for the denim crowd, but the ultramodern dining room will make you want to dress up and sip a martini. Beautiful plate presentations from chef Ryan Fancher, a French Laundry alum.

405 First Street West, Sonoma | 707/996-3030 | eldoradosonoma.com

HARVEST MOON CAFÉ

This Sonoma Plaza newcomer in a historic adobe has met with almost universal acclaim for Jen and Nick Demerest's Southern Mediterranean–accented menu, and for the casual grace of its setting, which includes an attractive back patio.

487 First Street West, Sonoma | 707/933-8160 | harvestmoonsonoma.com

LASALETTE RESTAURANT

Go here for earthy, delicious Portuguese dishes, with an emphasis on seafood.

452 First Street East, Suite H, Sonoma | 707/938-1927 | lasalette-restaurant.com

THE GIRL AND THE FIG

The girl is restaurateur/whirlwind Sondra Bernstein, whose bistro on the ground floor of the Sonoma Hotel is one of the best reasons to visit Sonoma Plaza. A new addition to Bernstein's empire, The Fig Pantry (1190 East Napa Street; 707/933-3000), is a few blocks away, next door to her Les Petites Maisons cottages.

110 West Spain Street, Sonoma | 707/938-3634 | thegirlandthefig.com

PLACES TO STAY

EL DORADO HOTEL

The modern (spare yet elegant decor) and the classic (a restored historic building right on Sonoma Plaza) mix nicely here. 28 rooms from $145.

405 First Street West, Sonoma | 707/996-3030 | hoteleldorado.com

EL PUEBLO INN

A favorite Sonoma bargain, this motel has old California style, a swimming pool, and reasonable rates. 53 rooms from $90.

896 West Napa Street, Sonoma | 707/996-3651 | elpuebloinn.com

FAIRMONT SONOMA MISSION INN

Maybe it's the rosé-pink buildings with their Cabernet-red tile roofs, but this resort just north of Sonoma has always seemed one of the most enjoyable of wine country retreats—at 10 acres big enough to be its own world, but convenient to valley wineries. 229 rooms from $290.

100 Boyes Boulevard, Sonoma | **707/938-9000** | **sonomamissioninn.com**

GAIGE HOUSE INN

This luxurious inn is considered one of the best in the Sonoma Valley. The setting —an 1890 Victorian in the center of Glen Ellen—is winning, rooms have been updated with great style, and the breakfasts are superb. 20 rooms from $195.

13540 Arnold Drive, Glen Ellen | **707/935-0237** | **gaige.com**

HOTEL LA ROSE

In Santa Rosa's Railroad Square, a century-old hotel with a beautiful stone façade; a contemporary addition is across the street. 47 rooms from $109.

308 Wilson Street, Santa Rosa | **800/527-6738** | **hotellarose.com**

INN AT SONOMA

This nicely appointed inn, part of the Four Sisters chain of boutique hotels, sits a couple of blocks from the Sonoma Plaza. 19 rooms from $145.

630 Broadway, Sonoma | **707/939-1340** | **innatsonoma.com**

KENWOOD INN AND SPA

Luxury, privacy, and sweeping views mark this small resort, which blends Tuscan architecture and California-style spa treatments. 32 rooms from $350.

10400 Sonoma Highway, Kenwood | **800/353-6966** | **kenwoodinn.com**

LEDSON HOTEL AND HARMONY CLUB

Project of Sonoma winemaker Steve Ledson, this intimate Sonoma Plaza hotel offers luxury and swing, thanks to regular jazz nights. 6 rooms from $350.

480 First Street East, Sonoma | **707/996-9779** | **ledsonhotel.com**

LES PETITES MAISONS

Newly opened by The Girl and the Fig doyenne Sondra Bernstein, these four whimsically but tastefully decorated cottages—each with kitchenette—are a real addition to the Sonoma lodging scene. 4 cottages from $125 a night.

1190 East Napa Street, Sonoma | **707/933-0340** | **thegirlandthefig.com**

VINTNERS INN

This plush inn is surrounded by a small vineyard, making it a fine place for travelers to soak up the Sonoma terroir. 44 rooms from $175.

4350 Barnes Road, Santa Rosa | **707/575-7350** | **vintnersinn.com**

DRY CREEK WINERIES

1 | SEGHESIO FAMILY VINEYARDS

At one point, the Seghesio family made most of the commercial-level wine in this county —more than a million-and-a-half gallons! Now, though, the fifth generation is focused on burnishing the legacy of their winemaking great-great-grandfather, Edoardo. Some of the Zinfandel they make today is from the vines Edoardo began planting at the turn of the last century. Taste with a view of the barrels, or bring some friends with you for a sit-down food-and-wine tasting on the weekend. Recipes include old family favorites, and some of the tables are made out of the winery's historic redwood tanks.

14730 Grove Street, Healdsburg | 707/433-3579 | seghesio.com

2 | RIDGE VINEYARDS

The Ridge Lytton Springs tasting room is innovative and kind to the environment in every way—earthen plaster over rice-straw bales let the walls breathe, computer-controlled louvers regulate the natural temperature, and solar panels generate about 75 percent of the winery's energy needs. Brainchild of Ridge Vineyards president Paul Draper—widely considered the dean of contemporary California winemaking—Lytton Springs is the winery's Zin-focused branch. Ahead of his time, Draper continues to capture the character of single vineyards by bottling many different Zins (all invariably wonderful).

650 Lytton Springs Road, Healdsburg | 707/433-7721 | ridgewine.com

3 | MAZZOCCO

You can see all the way to Mt. St. Helena from Mazzocco's new, tall-windowed tasting room. While winemaker Antoine Favero does produce some Zin, as you'd expect in this place, he also works with Bordeaux varieties—Cabernet, Merlot, Sauvignon Blanc—and Chardonnay, diversity worthy of his French birthplace and childhood sojourn in Peru.

1400 Lytton Springs Road, Healdsburg | 707/431-8159 | mazzocco.com

4 | AMPHORA WINERY

A former winemaker at Quivira, Rick Hutchinson is the artist behind Amphora now: The pots he throws, modeled after the clay vessels—amphorae—that the ancient Greeks and Romans used for wine, became the symbol for his own winery. After a bold, boot-strapping few years of winemaking in a prune barn (where he became known among the wine-touring underground for letting women stomp in his grapes), Hutchinson has moved up to this co-op complex, where he has a proper tasting room. Syrah, Zinfandel, Petite Sirah—they're all lush and balanced.

4791 Dry Creek Road, Healdsburg | 707/431-7767 | amphorawines.com

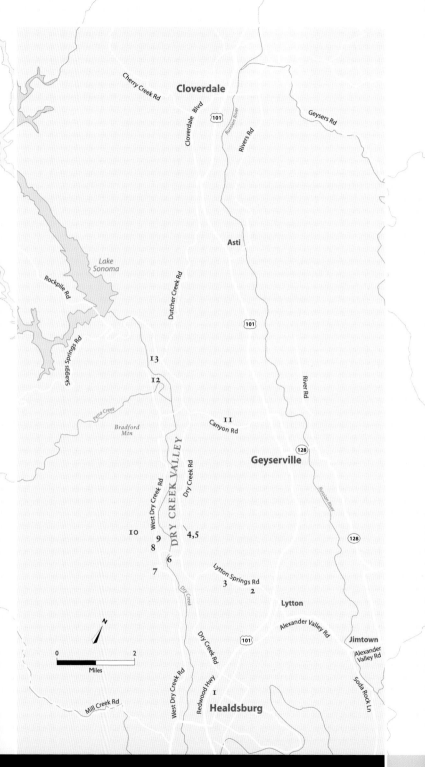

Cherry Creek Rd

Cloverdale

Cloverdale Blvd

Russian River

Rivers Rd

Geysers Rd

101

Asti

Dutcher Creek Rd

Lake Sonoma

Rockpile Rd

Skaggs Springs Rd

101

River Rd

I3

I2

Pena Creek

Bradford Mtn

I I

Canyon Rd

128

Geyserville

DRY CREEK VALLEY

West Dry Creek Rd

Dry Creek Rd

Russian River

I0

9

8

7

6

4,5

Dry Creek

Lytton Springs Rd

3

2

Lytton

Alexander Valley Rd

128

Jimtown

N

0   2

Miles

West Dry Creek Rd

Dry Creek Rd

101

Redwood Hwy

Alexander Valley Rd

Soda Rock Ln

I

Mill Creek Rd

West Dry Creek Rd

Healdsburg

5 | PAPAPIETRO PERRY WINERY

A project newly launched among former business associates and friends, Ben Papapietro and Bruce and Renae Perry, this winery has earned quick acclaim for its single-vineyard Pinot Noirs. You can taste them now at their copper-topped, barrel-stave bar in the same casual complex that houses Amphora Wines.

4791 Dry Creek Road, Healdsburg | 877/467-4668 | papapietro-perry.com

6 | DRY CREEK VINEYARD

The ivy-covered stone blocks of the winery make a grand backdrop for a picnic here, and the wines in the tasting room of this longtime Dry Creek player are getting better and better, thanks to a recent refocus on estate wines. A happy exception to "estate" here is Chenin Blanc—a great version of a wine we shouldn't lose, this one from Clarksburg in the Sacramento Delta. Stop in at the Dry Creek General Store on the corner for some sandwiches, then snag some Chenin and grab a table.

3770 Lambert Bridge Road, Healdsburg | 800/864-9463 | drycreekvineyard.com

7 | LAMBERT BRIDGE WINERY

On the edge of Zinfandel territory, Lambert Bridge somehow became known for Merlot and other Bordeaux varieties, although it does make some interesting vineyard-designated Zins. Turn left after crossing the old trestle bridge the winery was named for and you'll reach this auspicious spot against the eastern hills, with its warm-feeling tasting room (the fireplace must have something to do with that) and one of the loveliest gardens for picnicking in Dry Creek Valley.

4085 West Dry Creek Road, Healdsburg | 707/431-9600 | lambertbridge.com

8 | A. RAFANELLI

If you want a taste of true Dry Creek Valley Zinfandel, make an appointment to come here, where four generations of Rafanellis have grown the valley's signature grape. Of course, there are Cabernet and Merlot too, but the Zin is the story—and this one is not available in retail shops.

4685 West Dry Creek Road, Healdsburg | 707/433-1385 (call for appointment) | arafanelliwinery.com

9 | QUIVIRA VINEYARDS

Another great stop for classic Dry Creek Valley Zinfandel, plus Sauvignon Blanc that's a treat, all biodynamically farmed. At Quivira (pronounced key-VEER-ah), you can also see former owners Holly and Henry Wendt's collection of maps depicting the West Coast of North America as it appeared to cartographers from the 1500s to the 1800s.

4900 West Dry Creek Road, Healdsburg | 800/292-8339 | quivirawine.com

10 | MICHEL-SCHLUMBERGER WINE ESTATE

The gracious courtyard around a long pond, where loud bullfrogs make themselves known in season after dark, might be mistaken for a Spanish mission, but the wines lean more to France. The vineyards take advantage of tiny pocket valleys in the benchlands on the east side of Dry Creek, to produce elegant, structured Bordeaux varieties.

4155 Wine Creek Road, Healdsburg | 800/447-3060 (call for appointment) | michelschlumberger.com

11 | J. PEDRONCELLI WINERY

The J. stands for John, yet another of the early Italian immigrants to Dry Creek Valley, who bought his vineyards and winery in 1927. His sons John and Jim carried on the business for decades as winemaker and marketing director, respectively; the third generation only recently stepped to the fore. The single-vineyard wines show the winery at its best.

1220 Canyon Road, Geyserville | 707/857-3531 | pedroncelli.com

12 | PRESTON OF DRY CREEK

You'll find the casual, country side of winemaking here. Lou and Susan Preston are organic farmers as well as wine producers. Their products—olives, pickled veggies, hot sauce, and, if you are lucky, fresh bread—can be had in the tasting room.

9282 West Dry Creek Road, Healdsburg | 707/433-3372 | prestonvineyards.com

13 | FERRARI-CARANO VINEYARDS & WINERY

Solid Chardonnays and Sauvignon Blancs (labeled Fumé Blancs) are to be found here, in a grand arched and porticoed Italian setting. The five acres of formal gardens star. And in the new, ultracool underground Enoteca Reserve Tasting Bar, you can try some of Ferrari-Carano's very good single-vineyard wines.

8761 Dry Creek Road, Healdsburg | 707/433-6700 | ferrari-carano.com

FAVORITES & DISCOVERIES ☆ DRY CREEK

RIDGE VINEYARDS *An environmentally friendly Zin-focused winery from the dean of contemporary California winemaking*

AMPHORA WINERY *Winemaker Rick Hutchinson's Syrah, Zinfandel, and Petite Sirah are lush and balanced*

QUIVIRA VINEYARDS *A great stop for classic, biodynamically farmed Dry Creek Valley Zinfandel*

PRESTON OF DRY CREEK *Go here to experience Sonoma County in all its rural glory—from the organic veggies to the minimalist wine*

WHERE TO EAT

BARNDIVA

The menu requires some concentration—it's divided into Light, Spicy, and Comfort categories, forcing you to choose what mood you're in that day—but the food is good and the setting is lovely, especially the back patio.

231 Center Street, Healdsburg | 707/431-0100 | barndiva.com

BISTRO RALPH

One of the first places on the square to set the bar for excellent seasonal cuisine.

109 Plaza Street, Healdsburg | 707/433-1380

BOVOLO

Terrific pizza and salads, located behind Scharffen Berger chocolate and other gourmet food and wine stalls in the Plaza Farms complex.

106 Matheson Street, Healdsburg | 707/431-2962

CYRUS

Exquisite cooking that's giving Napa Valley's French Laundry a run for its money.

29 North Street, Healdsburg | 707/433-3311 | cyrusrestaurant.com

DOWNTOWN BAKERY & CREAMERY

Longtime favorite for morning (or anytime) pastries. Head baker and owner Kathleen Stewart is a Chez Panisse disciple.

308 A Center Street, Healdsburg | 707/431-2719 | downtownbakery.net

DRY CREEK GENERAL STORE

It sells fishing bait, a great selection of local wines, and sandwiches, from meat loaf to prosciutto di Parma with fresh mozzarella.

3495 Dry Creek Road, Healdsburg | 707/433-4171 | dcgstore.com

DRY CREEK KITCHEN

New York celebrity-chef Charlie Palmer opened this place, then moved to town. Local ingredients and wines are in good hands in this serene, classy dining room.

317 Healdsburg Avenue, Healdsburg | 707/431-0330 | charliepalmer.com/dry_creek

FLYING GOAT COFFEE

Just "the Goat" to locals, it serves excellent coffee and pastries.

324 Center Street, Healdsburg | 707/433-3599 | flyinggoatcoffee.com

JIMTOWN STORE

In the Alexander Valley just east of Healdsburg, Carrie Brown's Americana-filled general store is the place to stop for sublime sandwiches, salads, and what is without a doubt the world's best chocolate pudding.

6706 State Highway 128, Healdsburg | **707/433-1212** | **jimtown.com**

WILLI'S SEAFOOD & RAW BAR

An extension of the excellent Willi's Wine Bar near Santa Rosa (4404 Old Redwood Highway; 707/526-3096), this lively hangout serves Latin-leaning small plates.

403 Healdsburg Avenue, Healdsburg | **707/433-9191** | **willisseafood.net**

PLACES TO STAY

BEST WESTERN DRY CREEK INN

This popular motel has expanded, adding a 60-room "Tuscan-style" courtyard building. Not quaint, but pleasant and reasonably priced. 103 rooms from $89.

198 Dry Creek Road, Healdsburg | **707/433-0300** | **drycreekinn.com**

HOTEL HEALDSBURG

A jolt of the hip and haute-moderne in downtown Healdsburg, the celadon-green hotel looks ready for a spread in *Vogue*. 55 rooms from $260.

25 Matheson Street, Healdsburg | **800/889-7188** | **hotelhealdsburg.com**

HEALDSBURG INN ON THE PLAZA

As the name suggests, guests in this hotel can savor the activity on Healdsburg's charming central square. 12 rooms from $200.

112 Matheson Street, Healdsburg | **800/431-8663** | **healdsburginn.com**

LES MARS

The Loire arrives in Sonoma County, in the form of a French château near the plaza. Given the level of opulence, it makes perfect sense that Healdsburg's most acclaimed new restaurant, Cyrus, has its home here. 16 rooms from $475.

27 North Street, Healdsburg | **877/431-1700** | **lesmarshotel.com**

MADRONA MANOR

With its gables and mansard roof, this gorgeous inn defines Victorian-era splendor, and the surrounding 8 acres of gardens are lovely. The inn's Madrona Manor Restaurant is well regarded, with an exemplary wine list. 23 rooms from $210.

1001 Westside Road, Healdsburg | **800/258-4003** | **madronamanor.com**

ALEXANDER VALLEY WINERIES

1 | KENDALL-JACKSON WINE CENTER

Not strictly a tasting room or a visitor center—you might call this the seat of an empire. Wineries as diverse as Sonoma's Arrowood, Napa's Cardinale, and Santa Maria's Byron Vineyard now live in the portfolio of Jackson Family Wines. But in the landmark château that is the Kendall-Jackson Wine Center, you can taste the core brand with pairings from the executive chef, wander through the winemaking exhibits and extensive gardens, and picnic under fabulous old oaks.

5007 Fulton Road, Fulton | 707/571-8100 | kj.com

2 | CHALK HILL ESTATE

Rich in history and natural beauty, Chalk Hill is the primary winery in the tiny AVA of the same name, in the warmer, easternmost part of the Russian River Valley. Winegrowing dates back to the 1860s on the rolling hills surrounding the stone-and-wood estate. You can talk terrain and trellising on a viticulture tour, or do more than talk on a culinary tour that ends with small plates the chef creates from the winery's organic garden.

**10300 Chalk Hill Road, Healdsburg |
800/838-4306 (call for appointment) | chalkhill.com**

3 | ROSENBLUM CELLARS

Rosenblum is based in Alameda, but it has a tasting room just off the plaza in Healdsburg, which is a great place to compare a range of its Zin bottlings from different appellations, very close to where many of them are grown.

250 Center Street, Healdsburg | 707/431-1169 | rosenblumcellars.com

4 | GALLO FAMILY VINEYARDS

Gallo is a punching bag, a publicity machine, and—from its Modesto headquarters—responsible for an awful lot of swill in the world. But the Gallo of Sonoma division has focused on better quality, and offers great wines for the money. At its tasting room on the square in Healdsburg, you can choose from a whole menu of flights. Here you can also make reservations to tour one of its vineyards in the Alexander Valley.

320 Center Street, Healdsburg | 707/433-2458 | gallosonoma.com

5 | SOUVERAIN

Despite some confusing ownership changes, this large winery has consistently produced good-value Merlots and Cabs with all the great characteristics of Alexander Valley fruit, as well as a Chardonnay that shows off the Russian River. While you can't visit the property itself anymore, you can taste the wines in town.

**Cellar 360, 308 B Center Street, Healdsburg |
707/433-2822 | chateausouverain.com**

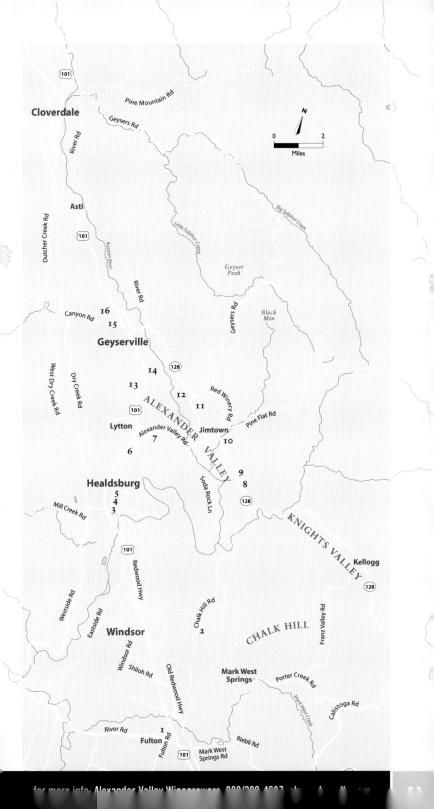

6 | SIMI

A proper visitor center has replaced the original champagne-tank tasting room at Simi, which spans much of California's winemaking history. Isabelle, daughter of one of the two Simi brothers who dug Simi's first stone cellar in 1880, continued to make (and cellar) wine through Prohibition, and worked in the winery even after she sold it in 1970. Today, Simi's Alexander Valley Cabernets do well by the region.

16275 Healdsburg Avenue, Healdsburg | 800/746-4880 | simiwinery.com

7 | JORDAN VINEYARD & WINERY

Jordan Cabernets reign over Alexander Valley from their grand French château with sweeping, wraparound views. One winemaker, Rob Davis, has stayed the course from the early days, when he worked with legendary winemaker André Tchelistcheff, for a wine that's always short-listed among California's most respected.

**1474 Alexander Valley Road, Healdsburg |
800/654-1213 (call for appointment) | jordanwinery.com**

8 | HANNA WINERY ALEXANDER VALLEY

Hanna's light-filled, Mediterranean-style tasting room is a wonderful Alexander Valley destination. Christine Hanna, daughter of founder Dr. Elias Hanna, is president. The Sauvignon Blanc here is one of the region's great ones; you can taste it at the regular bar, but make an appointment in the sit-down reserve area for a chance to try some stellar bottlings from the winery's high-elevation Bismark Ranch Vineyard.

9280 Highway 128, Healdsburg | 707/431-4310 | hannawinery.com

9 | ALEXANDER VALLEY VINEYARDS

On the original homestead of Cyrus Alexander, the valley's namesake settler, the Wetzel Family's Alexander Valley Vineyards led the way when this region began to be resettled by wineries three decades ago. The grounds and gardens around Cyrus's restored adobe house make a beautiful setting for a picnic, and the red blend named Cyrus shows what this warm valley can produce.

8644 Highway 128, Healdsburg | 800/888-7209 | avvwine.com

10 | SAUSAL WINERY

There are some very old vines behind Sausal's Zinfandels, and a lot of winemaking history in the story of the Demostene family, which founded and still owns Sausal. Before Prohibition, the grandfather of the current generation of Demostenes, Abele Ferrari, invented the Healdsburg Crusher. In 1956, Ferrari's daughter and son-in-law, Leo Demostene, bought Sausal Ranch, where Leo always wanted to convert an old prune dehydrator into a winemaking facility. His four children accomplished it.

7370 Highway 128, Healdsburg | 800/500-2285 | sausalwinery.com

I I | STRYKER SONOMA

The tasting room is enclosed on three sides by floor-to-ceiling glass walls, offering views down into the barrel room, the fermentation area, and the crush pad—not to mention a dramatic swath of the Alexander Valley and the Mayacamas Range.

5110 Highway 128, Geyserville | 800/433-1944 |
strykersonoma.com

I 2 | MURPHY-GOODE ESTATE WINERY

A lot of lively wines are poured at Murphy-Goode's marble bar, including a "Liar's Dice" Zinfandel made from grapes grown by late cofounder Tim Murphy's regular liar's dice buddies at Mickey's Café in nearby Geyserville. The winery's Fumé Blanc is a favorite.

4001 Highway 128, Geyserville | 707/431-7644 |
murphygoodewinery.com

I 3 | NEW, UNNAMED, COPPOLA WINERY

What's in a name? A lot, which is why at our press time Francis Ford Coppola was still pondering the right moniker for his newest project. He's purchased the former Chateau Souverain (which appears to have been built by Louis XIV but dates from the 1970s) and is using it to produce his Francis Coppola Presents, Francis Coppola Diamond Collection, and FC Reserve wines. Don't let the name issue deter you from visiting right now.

300 Via Archimedes, Geyserville | 707/857-1905 | ffcwinery.com

I 4 | CLOS DU BOIS

Winemaker Erik Olsen oversees this gargantuan operation in hands-on fashion, with the result that Clos du Bois wines are great values and fine examples of their respective sources, especially those from Alexander Valley. Don't miss Marlstone, Olsen's top Bordeaux blend, and Briarstone, which is 100 percent Cab.

19411 Geyserville Avenue, Geyserville | 800/222-3189 |
closdubois.com

I 5 | GEYSER PEAK WINERY

Nothing short of an institution, Geyser Peak has had its ups and downs through more than a century's worth of winemaking. But its wines are better than ever and great values—the Sauvignon Blanc makes a fine house white.

22281 Chianti Road, Geyserville | 800/255-9463 |
geyserpeakwinery.com

I 6 | SILVER OAK CELLARS

Legendary Silver Oak is usually identified with Napa, but much of its prized Cabernet Sauvignon comes from Alexander Valley, and it's more fun to taste it here.

24625 Chianti Road, Geyserville | 800/273-8809 | silveroak.com

RUSSIAN RIVER WINERIES

1 | RODNEY STRONG VINEYARDS

A dancer in his early life, Rodney Strong was a shaping force in Sonoma winemaking, advocating vineyard designation and other practices that are now a matter of course.

11455 Old Redwood Highway, Healdsburg | 707/431-1533 | rodneystrong.com

2 | J VINEYARDS & WINERY

For the sake of making sparkling wine, Judy Jordan, daughter of Tom Jordan, spun a winery off the house of Jordan, and called it…J. The bubbles have been joined by very good still Pinot Noir, Chardonnay, Pinot Gris, and food pairings in the tasting room.

11447 Old Redwood Highway, Healdsburg | 888/594-6326 | jwine.com

3 | ROSHAMBO WINERY

Roshambo hits the "cool" spot in all of us, with its spectacular concrete-and-glass design. Owner Naomi Johnson Brilliant aims to pull in a diverse crowd in the airy, arty space.

3000 Westside Road, Healdsburg | 888/525-9463 | roshambowinery.com

4 | DAVIS BYNUM WINERY

There's a dark woodsiness about the setting at Davis Bynum. The winery has an innovative permaculture garden, built on a multifaceted, sustainable growing system, and the Pinots, from various Russian River vineyards, are invariably interesting.

8075 Westside Road, Healdsburg | 800/826-1073 | davisbynum.com

5 | GARY FARRELL VINEYARDS & WINERY

The tasting bar is perched above the wildest part of the valley, where evergreens and oaks ring vineyard-wrapped knolls. This is a Pinot house, so come to compare.

10701 Westside Road, Healdsburg | 707/473-2900 | garyfarrellwines.com

10 | HARTFORD FAMILY WINERY

This grand-scale château houses some equally showy wines. Compare high-end single-vineyard Russian River Pinots with ones from other regions.

8075 Martinelli Road, Forestville | 707/887-1756 | hartfordwines.com

7 | IRON HORSE RANCH AND VINEYARDS

Sidle up to the tasting planks slung across barrels out in front of the corral, grab a flute of bubbles, and revel in the view. Iron Horse makes refined but expressive sparkling wines from the exciting Green Valley AVA, but its still wines are stealing attention.

9786 Ross Station Road, Sebastopol | 707/887-1507 | ironhorsevineyards.com

8 | DE LOACH VINEYARDS

Long known for making a host of different wines, De Loach is now owned by a French winemaking family, which is focusing on improving its Pinot, Chard, and Zin.

1791 Olivet Road, Santa Rosa | 707/526-9111 | deloachvineyards.com

9 | MARIMAR ESTATE

Marimar Torres has tucked a gracious Spanish bodega among her vineyards in a remote corner of Green Valley, and is making lovely Pinot Noir and Chardonnay.

11400 Graton Road, Sebastopol | 707/823-4365 | marimarestate.com

10 | DUTTON-GOLDFIELD WINERY

Partners Steve Dutton (grower) and Dan Goldfield (winemaker) have been producing ever-more-striking Russian River Valley Pinot Noirs and Chardonnays in recent years.

5700 Occidental Road, Santa Rosa | 707/568-2455 | duttongoldfield.com

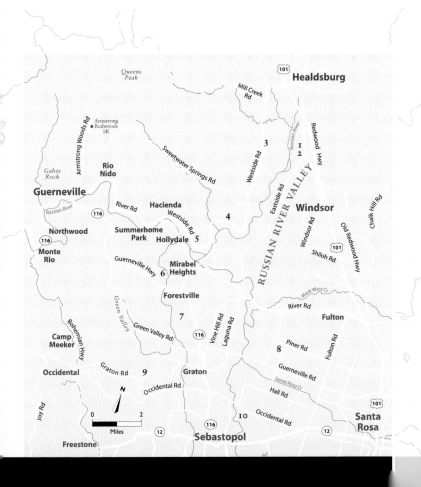

THINGS TO DO

ARMSTRONG REDWOODS STATE RESERVE AND
AUSTIN CREEK STATE RECREATION AREA

Armstrong has towering coast redwoods alongside the Russian River. Beside it is Austin Creek State Recreation Area, whose more open terrain has camp sites.

17000 Armstrong Woods Road, Guerneville | 707/869-2015

CANOE AND KAYAK

Generations of Northern Californians have first put paddle to water here on the Russian River. Outfitters include **Burke's Canoe Trips** (8600 River Road, Forestville; 707/887-1222; burkescanoetrips.com), **River's Edge Canoe and Kayak** (13840 Healdsburg Avenue, Healdsburg; 800/345-0869; riversedgekayakandcanoe.com), and **SOAR** (20 Healdsburg Avenue, Healdsburg; 707/433-5599; soar1.com).

FARM TRAILS

While vineyards have displaced some of Sonoma County's fabled fruit orchards, the county is still a paradise for the fresh produce lover. The largest concentration of growers are in the Sebastopol and Russian River areas.

Sonoma County Farm Trails | 800/207-9464 | farmtrails.org

OSMOSIS

If your idea of heaven is a cedar enzyme bath followed by a Zen harmony facial, then this soothing Asian-influenced day spa is the place for you.

209 Bohemian Highway, Freestone | 707/823-8231 | osmosis.com

WHERE TO EAT

KOZLOWSKI FARMS

Jam-lovers have long made pilgrimages to this Russian River landmark.

5566 Highway 116, Forestville | 800/473-2767 | kozlowskifarms.com

MOSAIC RESTAURANT & WINE LOUNGE

Yummy elements are layered exuberantly in every dish at this Forestville outpost.

6675 Front Street, Forestville | 707/887-7503 | mosaiceats.com

RESTAURANT MIREPOIX

Chef-owner Matthew Bousquet makes the most of local market produce.

275 Windsor River Road, Windsor | 707/838-0162 | restaurantmirepoix.com

SCREAMING MIMI'S

Man- and womankind does not live by Cabernet alone; sometimes we want a double Peanut Butter Fudge Twirl on a waffle cone. When that urge hits, call Mimi.

6902 Sebastopol Avenue, Sebastopol | 707/823-5902

SOPHIE'S WINE CELLARS

A superior wine store, with lots of hard-to-find vintages from the Russian River and Sonoma Coast. Cheeses and breads, too.

20293 Highway 116, Monte Rio | 707/865-1122 | sophiescellars.com

PLACES TO STAY

APPLEWOOD

This rambling inn is a choice spot for touring the Russian River wine country. Also here is the superb Applewood restaurant. 19 rooms from $185.

13555 Highway 116, Guerneville | 800/555-8509 | applewoodinn.com

THE FARMHOUSE INN

You get privacy and considerable luxury at an inn that began life as a 19th-century farmhouse. The inn's Farmhouse Restaurant is terrific. 8 rooms from $250.

7871 River Road, Forestville | 800/464-6642 | farmhouseinn.com

HOPE-BOSWORTH HOUSE AND HOPE-MERRILL HOUSE

The Hope-Merrill House began life in the 1870s as a stagecoach stop; the Hope-Bosworth House is a less formal Craftsman-style home. 12 rooms from $129.

21253 Geyserville Avenue, Geyserville | 800/825-4233 | hope-inns.com

INN AT OCCIDENTAL

Extremely appealing 1877 Victorian. 16 rooms from $199.

3657 Church Street, Occidental | 800/522-6324 | innatoccidental.com

RIDENHOUR RANCH HOUSE INN

Tucked among the Russian River redwoods, a 1906-vintage farmhouse is now a relaxed, reasonably priced retreat. 8 rooms from $139.

12850 River Road, Guerneville | 888/877-4466 | ridenhourinn.com

SEBASTOPOL INN

A handsome hotel in an increasingly interesting town. 31 rooms from $138.

6751 Sebastopol Avenue, Sebastopol | 800/653-1082 | sebastopolinn.com

MENDOCINO

MENDOCINO COUNTY MARKS California wine country's northern frontier. Here is where the state's mainly Mediterranean climate confronts the wetter Pacific Northwest. Valleys are greener, mountains steeper and more thickly covered with pine and fir. On the other side of the Coast Range runs the Mendocino shore in all its rocky splendor: You can't see it, but you sense its stormy presence. Roads narrow, winter skies turn slate-gray and loose rainstorms that swell the Russian and Navarro rivers in their banks. Vineyards are tucked between stands of coast redwoods and meadows of grazing sheep. Winemaking tends toward the intimate and idiosyncratic, and is very clearly shaped by the natural world.

Of the 50 county wineries drawing from 15,500 acres of vineyards across eight AVAs (with two more proposed), the most newsworthy are in remote Anderson Valley, running along State Highway 128 north from Boonville through Philo, until it dives into the redwoods on its way to the sea. Where the Navarro River breaks through the trees, the ocean fog rolls in, establishing the valley as Pinot Noir territory. Look no further than Navarro Vineyards, masters of the Pinot craft, for evidence. Navarro also offers testimony to the region's white-wine strength—its cool-weather Gewürztraminer and Riesling are coming on strong.

The French took note of the Anderson Valley back in the 1980s, when none other than Roederer saw the potential for Pinot Noir and Chardonnay—the two main grapes in Champagne—and established one of the best sparkling-wine houses in California. More recently, Napa winemakers have begun infiltrating, among them Duckhorn's immensely civilized (for these parts) Goldeneye.

Continues page 62 >

SUGGESTED ROUTES

☆ **HIGHWAY 128** For one of the best wine drives in California, leave Highway
101 in Cloverdale and follow Highway 128 as it twists and turns up to
Yorkville, then leads you down into the Anderson Valley, Boonville, and Philo.
From here you can continue to the Mendocino coast, or return the way
you came.

☆ **HIGHWAY 101** The stretch of 101 from Hopland to Ukiah is dotted with
easily accessed wineries. Branch east on Highway 20 to hit the wineries of
Redwood Valley.

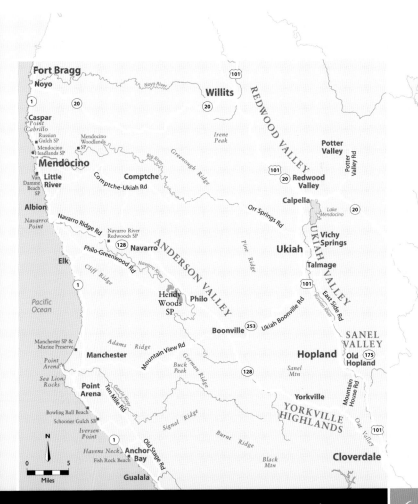

The valley floor is not the whole Anderson Valley story though. There's a stealth region above the fog, Mendocino Ridge, unique as an AVA in being a noncontiguous collection of peaks that reach above the 1,400-foot fog line to produce warmth-loving Zinfandel from vineyards planted by Italian immigrants in the late 1800s. The southern entrance to the valley also has its own appellation, the Yorkville Highlands, where interesting, organic winemaking abounds.

Inland, the wine story has been shaped in a very big way by the very big Fetzer family. In the 1960s, Barney and Kathleen Fetzer rode the modern wine boom—or maybe launched it—first from their Home Ranch in Redwood Valley, then from vineyards near Hopland, eventually producing an astonishing number of cases a year. Many of their 11 children worked in the business and joined forces to run it after Barney's death. In 1992, the family sold the enormous operation to Brown-Forman Corporation—and now that the non-compete period has ended, many of the siblings are getting right back to winemaking.

For the traveler, Mendocino divides itself neatly into two regions: the wineries along State Highway 128 and those along U.S. Highway 101. Running from Hopland north through Ukiah to Redwood Valley, Highway 101 takes you to the wineries of the upper Russian River area— the Sanel, Ukiah, and Redwood valleys. Some of these wineries, like Jepson and Jericho, lie just off the highway. Others, like Fife, require detours over pretty country roads.

Along the way, the town of Hopland has a couple of good hotels and is becoming a center for winery tasting rooms. The area clearly misses the presence of the now-closed Fetzer Valley Oaks Hospitality Center east of town, but you can still have a good time here. Farther north, Ukiah— the county seat—is something of a sleeper. It has a picturesque location at the base of the Coast Range, a first-class cultural attraction (the Grace Hudson Museum), and a downtown filled with handsome early-20th-century buildings. Now it's beginning to get the restaurants it needs to become a wine-country destination.

As for the Anderson Valley, perhaps the most important thing to note is how protective residents and visitors alike are about it. People don't want it to change, and after one visit you understand why. It is perfect as it is. There are a dozen or so wineries, all of them of interest, a good hotel with a great restaurant, and a couple of bed and breakfasts, but one should underline all the things that aren't here: spa resorts, tasting rooms modeled after Versailles, doggy boutiques, balloon rides. That leaves room to enjoy the rolling vineyards, the turns of the Navarro River, the redwoods at Hendy Woods, the green hills with the darker green mountains beyond. At its best, wine tasting makes you appreciate not just a wine but the things that give us that wine—soil, rain, sun, sky. Wine tasting in the Anderson Valley does precisely that.

HIGHWAY 128 WINERIES

1 | YORKVILLE CELLARS

This namesake winery in the small Yorkville Highlands AVA is committed to certified-organic wines, with good results. Nab a bottle of Viognier in the tasting room tucked under the trees, and take it out to the coast in search of some Dungeness crab.

25701 Highway 128, Yorkville | 707/894-9177 | yorkvillecellars.com

2 | MAPLE CREEK WINERY

Linda Stutz and Tom Rodriguez, Marin County refugees, have found a life they love at Maple Creek. You can taste their Artevino wines in a rustic ranch building off the main highway. And if they invite you to stay for one of their legendary weekend parties, you might find yourself drinking bubbly out of the navel of someone lying on the bar.

20799 Highway 128, Yorkville | 707/895-3001 | maplecreekwine.com

3 | MEYER FAMILY CELLARS

This attractive Mendocino-modern (lots of dark wood) tasting room is plunked down in a pretty valley off Highway 128. The late co-founder, Justin Meyer, also co-founded Napa's respected Silver Oak Cellars, where he spent 28 years. Now son Matt is focusing on Syrah and Port—since the Meyers feel the latter goes especially well with chocolate, tastings are accompanied by a piece or two of Scharffen Berger.

19750 Highway 128, Yorkville | 707/895-2341 | mfcellars.com

4 | CLAUDIA SPRINGS WINERY

Transplants from the San Jose area, Claudia and Bob Klindt started this small operation with a Chardonnay in 1989. Now their Zinfandels and estate Pinot Noirs are getting attention. You can taste them—along with the wines of Raye's Hill and Philo Ridge—in the yellow Anderson Valley Wine Experience building across from the Boonville Hotel.

2160 Guntly Road, Philo | 707/895-3926 | claudiasprings.com

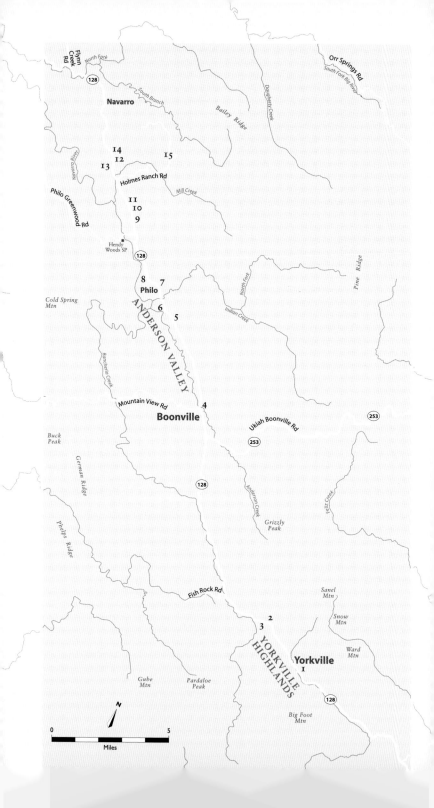

5 | BREGGO CELLARS

Sonoma-bred Douglas Ian Stewart founded and sold an Amazonian fruit sorbet company before coming home to realize his lifelong dream of starting a winery. Observing Stewart's passion for Breggo is part of the fun of visiting this modest tasting room, a yellow barn between Boonville and Philo. Breggo means "sheep" in Boontling, the native patois of the Anderson Valley, hence the horned beast on the label.

11001 Highway 128, Boonville | 707/895-9589 | breggo.com

6 | GOLDENEYE

Before Goldeneye, Anderson Valley wine tasting was strictly backroads-casual. This branch of Napa's Duckhorn Wine Company—a definite sign that deep pockets see great promise in this valley—raises the bar on tasting-room treatment. Sip a glass of the slightly lower-priced Migration or the full-on rich Goldeneye Pinot on the back terrace, which overlooks the lovely grounds and rolling swaths of vineyards fading to the redwoods beyond, and it's hard to see why any of this is a problem.

9200 Highway 128, Philo | 707/895-3202 | goldeneyewinery.com

7 | SCHARFFENBERGER CELLARS

Founded by John Scharffenberger, who subsequently sold the winery and went on to chocolate fame, Scharffenberger Cellars became Pacific Echo, then Scharffenberger Cellars again. But whatever it's been called, the winery has earned a reputation for great value, tasty sparkling wine, and a vibrant art-filled tasting room.

8501 Highway 128, Philo | 707/895-2957

8 | BRUTOCAO CELLARS

The Anderson Valley tasting room shows off the rustic side of Brutocao—the sleeker side being their newer tasting center in Hopland. Both offer interesting goods to purchase along with wine. The Hopland center includes exhibits on local history (old photographs, high school sports uniforms) and you can grab a meal at the adjacent Crushed Grape cafe.

7000 Highway 128, Philo | 707/895-2152 | brutocaocellars.com

9 | NAVARRO VINEYARDS

The appealing Navarro tasting room is the hub of Anderson Valley wine traffic. There's a spirit of generosity about the way the staff pours any wines of choice from the fairly long list of beautifully crafted Pinot Noirs, Rieslings, and Gewürztraminers (one of California's great ones). Buy a bottle of "méthode à l'ancienne" Pinot and some smoked salmon from the deli case, carry them out to one of the tables under the arbor, and experience what California wine touring is all about.

5601 Highway 128, Philo | 800/537-9463 | navarrowine.com

10 | GREENWOOD RIDGE VINEYARDS

Neighbor to Navarro, the octagonal Greenwood Ridge tasting room—designed by owner Allan Green's father, Aaron Green, who worked with Frank Lloyd Wright for many years—offers wraparound valley views. The vineyards themselves are at 1,400 feet in the Mendocino Ridge appellation; compare wines from these unique vineyards with those from the heart of the valley. Also, don't miss Greenwood Ridge's rather hilarious annual California Wine Tasting Championships each July.

5501 Highway 128, Philo | **707/895-2002** | **greenwoodridge.com**

11 | LAZY CREEK VINEYARDS

Possibly the most down-home winery in the valley—Josh Chandler might pour you some juice right out of the barrel in the cellar that serves as a tasting room. Lazy Creek Gewürztraminer is revered among aficionados for its bone-dry Alsatian style, and the Pinot is darned good too. The drive up the winding, dirt road through oak woodlands is part of the fun.

4741 Highway 128, Philo | **707/895-3623 (call for appointment)** | **lazycreekvineyards.com**

12 | ROEDERER ESTATE

The French Champagne house Louis Roederer knew a good thing when they saw the Anderson Valley in the early 1980s. From their large (for this region, anyway) Pinot and Chardonnay vineyards, they make sparkling wine that is consistently among the best in the state. The drive up to the winery sweeps around the vineyards and puts you in a tasting room with grand views behind the bar—after sipping some bubbly, move on to their rarer still wine.

4501 Highway 128, Philo | **707/895-2288** | **roedererestate.net**

13 | HUSCH VINEYARDS

The oldest winery in Anderson Valley is still charmingly rustic—the tiny rose-wrapped tasting room is housed in an old farm building, and sheep are used to keep weeds and grass below the grape vines trimmed. Sipping wine here often includes the opportunity to compare single varieties made into very different styles of wine.

4400 Highway 128, Philo | **800/554-8724** | **huschvineyards.com**

14 | HANDLEY CELLARS

Well-traveled winemaker Milla Handley, an earnest advocate for sustainable wine-growing methods, has filled her tasting room with folk art from around the world, and often pairs her wines with international food. The courtyard is a lovely place for a picnic.

3151 Highway 128, Philo | **800/733-3151** | **handleycellars.com**

15 | ESTERLINA VINEYARDS

A 2-mile drive off Highway 128 will yield great views, a lovely picnic spot, and wines from one of the smallest AVAs in the state—Cole Ranch, the only vineyard Esterlina owns.

1200 Holmes Ranch Road, Philo | 707/895-2920 | esterlinavineyards.com

HIGHWAY 101 WINERIES

1 | GRAZIANO FAMILY OF WINES

There are three branches in the Graziano "family": Domaine Saint Gregory, for Burgundian varietals; Monte Volpe and Enotria for Italian; and Graziano for hearty Mendocino reds, including Zinfandel. The Domaine Saint Gregory Pinot Noir is a consistently good value, and its location on the highway makes Graziano an easy stop.

13251 South Highway 101, Suite 3, Hopland | 707/744-8466 | grazianofamilyofwines.com

2 | MCDOWELL VALLEY VINEYARDS

The McDowell family's vineyards in the McDowell Valley east of Hopland are their own AVA, one of the first in this region. Syrah and Grenache have been growing here for almost a century, and the McDowells have continued the focus on Rhône grapes. The vibe in their new tasting room might suggest the Wild West, but the Syrah is all France, and the Viognier is mighty yummy.

13380 South Highway 101, Hopland | 707/744-8911 | mcdowellsyrah.com

3 | JERIKO ESTATE

One of the few "showcase" facilities in this casual county, Mediterranean-style Jeriko, about a mile north of Hopland, was built by Dan Fetzer, one of the many siblings in the Fetzer family. The wines are all from the organic and biodynamic estate vineyards—there's even a sparkler, which might be the only one in the state made from organic grapes. The tasting room is large and pleasant, and the patio is great for a picnic.

12141 Hewlitt & Sturtevant Road, Hopland | 707/744-1140 | jerikoestate.com

4 | SARACINA

Another new project from the Fetzer clan—this time it's John and his wife, Patty Rock. With caves blasted into the hill (the first ones in the county), master winemaker David Ramey on board, and Malbec thrown into its very interesting Atrea "Old Soul" red blend of Syrah, Zinfandel, and Petite Sirah, add Saracina to the list of achievements from this renowned Mendocino winemaking family.

11684 South Highway 101, Hopland | 707/744-1671 (call for appointment) | saracina.com

5 | JEPSON VINEYARDS

The large, white, porched Jepson is an unusual one-stop source for still wines, sparkling wines, and brandy—it's maybe the only winery in the United States that makes all three. The Sauvignon Blanc is the real star here.

10400 South Highway 101, Ukiah | 800/516-7342 | jepsonwine.com

6 | PARDUCCI WINE CELLARS

More than any other wine-family name, Parducci is synonymous with Mendocino County. Through years of different ownership, the label came to mean generally commercial-level wines, but now it's owned by the Mendocino Wine Company, which is committed to quality as well as organic and biodynamic practices. You can taste the results at the rustic, Western-feeling Parducci Wine Cellars just north of Ukiah, or at the Mendocino Wine Company tasting room on Main Street in the town of Mendocino.

501 Parducci Road, Ukiah | 888/362-9463 | parducci.com

7 | BARRA OF MENDOCINO

Charlie Barra has been growing grapes in this county for more than 50 years, and his wife, Martha, is a beloved spokesperson for local organic growing. They share the Redwood Valley Cellars facility with Braren Pauli wines. The round brick building is quaint and comfy but grand at the same time (with a fountain in the middle of the tasting room), and a cold bottle of their Muscat Canneli would go down easy at one of the garden tables on a hot day.

7051 North State Street, Redwood Valley | 707/485-0322 | barraofmendocino.com

8 | FIFE VINEYARDS

Dennis Fife has a Napa Valley vineyard on Spring Mountain, but some of his most exciting wines are the Rhône varieties and Zinfandels from his vineyards here in Redwood Valley—especially the Redhead Vineyard. (The "Redhead" in question is Karen MacNeil, who wrote the introduction to this book, is a longtime *Sunset* contributor, and is married to Dennis.) The homelike tasting room here offers grand views of Lake Mendocino, with a picnic-spot perch to enjoy them.

3620 Road B, Redwood Valley | 707/485-0323 | fifevineyards.com

9 | LOLONIS WINERY

This Greek winemaking family has given a symbol to their commitment to organic methods: the ladybug. Millions are released over their vines every summer to manage pests, and now the name is on a couple of their great-value blends.

1905 Road D, Redwood Valley | 707/485-7544 (call for appointment) | lolonis.com

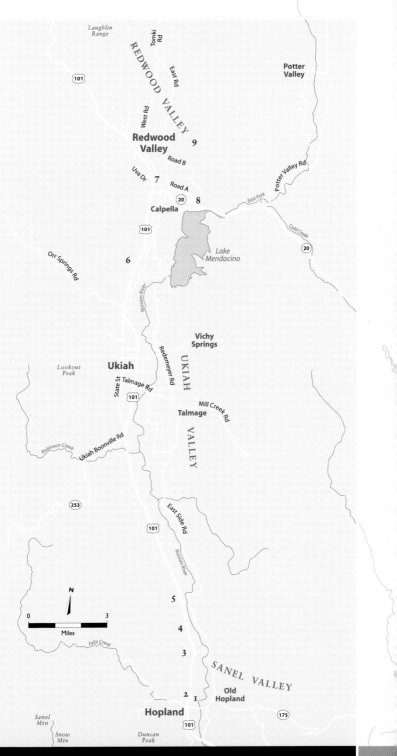

THINGS TO DO

ANDERSON VALLEY BREWING COMPANY

An outpost of foam in the valley of wine, the brewing company is an amiable stop, with tours and tastings of Boont Amber and other ales.

17700 Highway 253, Boonville | 707/895-2337 | avbc.com

THE APPLE FARM

Along with heirloom apples (try Pride of Philo) and assorted ciders and vinegars, The Apple Farm offers cooking classes and guest cottages for rent.

18501 Greenwood Road, Philo | 707/895-2333 | philoapplefarm.com

GOWAN'S OAK TREE

'Neath the spreading oak tree is a stand filled with apples and pears and vegetables in season, and cider and jams year-round.

6600 Highway 128, Philo | 707/895-3353

GRACE HUDSON MUSEUM AND SUN HOUSE

Ukiah's pride and joy, the museum honors artist Hudson and the collection of Native American art and artifacts she amassed, including Pomo basketry.

431 South Main Street, Ukiah | 707/467-2836 | gracehudsonmuseum.org

VICHY SPRINGS

Opened in 1852, its guests have included Mark Twain and Teddy Roosevelt. Today you can soak in one of the naturally carbonated mineral baths and stay the night.

2605 Vichy Springs Road, Ukiah | 707/462-9515 | vichysprings.com

WHERE TO EAT

BLUEBIRD CAFE

Any roadside cafe with a neon sign saying "EAT" had better serve darned good homemade pie, and in this the Bluebird delivers. If they have the coconut cream, count yourself a lucky traveler. Good eggs and burgers, too.

13340 South Highway 101, Hopland | 707/744-1633

LAUREN'S

A simpler alternative to The Boonville Hotel, Lauren's has an eclectic menu—burgers, pasta, Mexican—and a pleasing casual atmosphere.

14211 Highway 128, Boonville | 707/895-3869

PATRONA BISTRO AND WINE BAR

A shot of sophistication for downtown Ukiah: The urbane setting, the menu that reflects Mendocino's seasons, and the good wine list make Patrona a winner.

130 West Standley, Ukiah | 707/462-9181 | patronarestaurant.com

UKIAH BREWING COMPANY & RESTAURANT

Pilsners and burgers, all certified organic, and live music in downtown Ukiah.

102 South State Street, Ukiah | 707/468-5898 | ukiahbrewingco.com

PLACES TO STAY

HOPLAND INN AND RESTAURANT

Easily the grandest building in downtown Hopland. 21 rooms from $99.

13401 South Highway 101, Hopland | 800/266-1891 | hoplandinn.com

LAWSON'S STATION

On the edge of town, a modern Mediterranean-style inn. 7 rooms from $199.

13441 South Highway 101, Hopland | 707/744-1977 | lawsonsstation.com

THE BOONVILLE HOTEL

Blends 1860s history with Zen-like elegance. Dinner here makes the perfect ending to a day of wine tasting in the Anderson Valley. 8 rooms from $125.

14050 Highway 128, Boonville | 707/895-2210 | boonvillehotel.com

SPOTLIGHT THE MENDOCINO COAST

Forty minutes northwest of Anderson Valley is one of the most fabled shores in California. Everyone loves the Mendocino coast—for the drama of ocean batting against headlands and coves, for the prim New England grace of the town of Mendocino, for the coast's tourist buzz in summer and its stormy solitude in winter. ☆ You can eat and sleep very well in Mendocino proper. For dining, try **Cafe Beaujolais** *(961 Ukiah Street; 707/937-5614; cafebeaujolais.com).* **Joshua Grindle Inn** *(44800 Little Lake Road; 800/474-6353; joshuagrindleinn.com) is a great place to stay. One spot that shines at both is* **MacCallum House Inn and Restaurant** *(45020 Albion Street; 800/609-0492; maccallumhouse.com).*

LAKE

SAY LAKE COUNTY to most Northern Californians and they will think waterskiing on Clear Lake, concerts at Konocti Harbor, and very hot summers. Will they think wine? Probably not. This is a mistake. Lake County, whose grape history reaches back to the 19th century, is becoming one of California's more intriguing new centers of winemaking.

Just over the mountains from Calistoga, Lake County is classic interior California, a landscape of high, rounded, oak-studded hills. It is dominated by an extinct volcano, Mount Konocti, which rises 4,300 feet behind Kelseyville, and 68-square-mile Clear Lake, which is the largest freshwater lake entirely within California. (Take that, Lake Tahoe!)

It's also a good place for wine grapes. British actress Lillie Langtry didn't know that when she bought 22,000 acres in the Guenoc Valley sight-unseen in 1888 and began planting grapes, but nature was in her favor. Since then, a handful of others have discovered that Lake County has the microclimates, soils, and elevations for growing good wine grapes. Jed Steele, former winemaker for the Kendall-Jackson empire, voted for the region in 1991 when he founded Steele Wines on the south shore. And as you'd expect from a wine region next door to Mendocino, Lake County has a Fetzer—Jim, whose biodynamic Ceàgo vineyards, hacienda-style winery, and high-end resort (still in the works as we went to press) on the north shore promises to raise many bars.

Tourism here has always centered around the lake, with the lakeside towns—Lakeport, Kelseyville, Clearlake—crowded with bait shops and mom-and-pop resorts. Wine touring has been something you did in between swimming or boating. The county has fewer than a dozen wineries open for tasting, but a growing number are as elegant as anything in Napa (check out Brassfield Estates, open by appointment near Clearlake Oaks). Hotels like the Tallman in Upper Lake and restaurants like the Saw Shop in Kelseyville are likewise upping the ante for food and lodging. In short, Lake County is still a place where you'll want to bring your bathing suit and fishing rod, but don't ignore the wine.

SUGGESTED ROUTES

☆ **AROUND CLEAR LAKE** *Lake County's wineries are scattered around the lake, which is circled by Highways 29 (which leads south to Napa Valley) and 20 (which leads west to Ukiah and Highway 101). The towns of Upper Lake or Nice make good bases for visiting Ceàgo. Steele and Wildhurst are right in Kelseyville, and Langtry is the most far-flung in Middletown. But distances are short enough that you can catch most of the wineries in a day of tasting.*

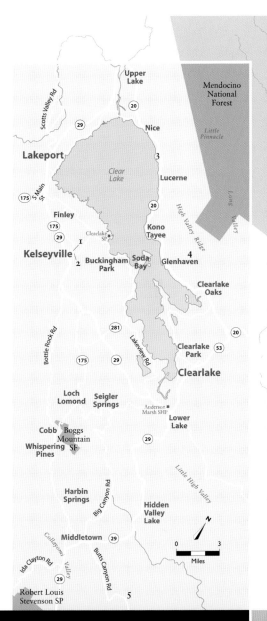

LAKE WINERIES

1 | STEELE WINES

Lake County's biggest and oldest boutique winery is worth a stop if you're looking for quality wines at a good value. Jed Steele put Kendall-Jackson on the map (bet you didn't know KJ started in Lake County) and he still produces great wines. Try the citrusy Sauvignon Blanc. A farmer's market sets up shop in the winery's grassy garden on Saturdays from May through October.

4350 Thomas Drive, Kelseyville | 707/279-9475 | steelewines.com

2 | WILDHURST VINEYARDS

The Holdenried family goes way back with the region's former main ag product, pears. Now they've added vineyards to their orchards, as well as a winery to produce their own label. You can taste the rather remarkable lineup in their homey, birch-floored tasting room in the restored Odd Fellows Hall on Kelseyville's main street. The Sauvignon Blanc is a great representation of the region's best grape to date.

3855 Main Street, Kelseyville | 707/279-4302 | wildhurst.com

3 | CEÀGO DEL LAGO

Already a gracious Mexican hacienda–style winery with its own dock (the only boat-in winery in the country, as far as owner Jim Fetzer knows), Ceàgo Del Lago is on its way to becoming a spectacular lakefront resort. The former owner of Fetzer Vineyards has developed a biodynamic farm here, running sheep through the vineyards when there's no green on the vines, chickens when there is. You can visit the tasting room now, but at press time a restaurant and lakeside villas were still in the offing.

5115 East Highway 20, Nice | 707/274-1462 | ceago.com

4 | BRASSFIELD ESTATE WINERY

This is a glorious spot, with views of Mount Konocti and myriad hills, dales, and micro-climates in between. Brassfield, on a former cattle ranch, is the main player in Lake County's newest AVA, High Valley. A grand facility in a distinctly nongrandiose region, Brassfield is matching the scale in its wines. Try the Syrahs.

**10915 High Valley Road, Clearlake Oaks |
707/998-1895 (call for appointment) | brassfieldestate.com**

5 | LANGTRY ESTATE & VINEYARDS

Formerly Guenoc, the 22,000-acre Langtry property has reassociated itself with its first owner, the flamboyant 19th-century British theater star Lillie Langtry. Besides history and a yummy Petite Sirah, come here for the summer film festival and other events.

21000 Butts Canyon Road, Middletown | 707/987-2385 | langtryestate.com

THINGS TO DO

CLEAR LAKE QUEEN

Sail the lake and dine in style on a replica paddlewheel steamboat.

9190 Soda Bay Road, Kelseyville | **707/994-5432**

SEELY RANCH

From August through November, the ranch's farm stand just off Highway 20 is a homey place to taste Lake County's nonwine bounty, notably its famous pears.

Highway 20, Upper Lake | **707/275-9250**

WHERE TO EAT

BLUE HERON CAFE

This classic California Mexican/American cafe in "downtown" Upper Lake serves eggs over easy or huevos rancheros for breakfast, burgers or burritos for lunch.

9475 Main Street, Upper Lake | **707/275-9021**

BLUE WING SALOON CAFE

This newcomer next door to the Tallman Hotel looks like a small-town saloon, but the beef and pastas are adroitly done, and the roster of local wines is impressive.

9520 Main Street, Upper Lake | **707/275-2233** | **bluewingsaloon.com**

SAW SHOP GALLERY BISTRO

It's a pretty little art-filled bungalow in downtown Kelseyville, with an eclectic menu and monthly winemaker dinners that spotlight local wineries.

3825 Main Street, Kelseyville | **707/278-0129** | **sawshopbistro.com**

PLACES TO STAY

KONOCTI HARBOR RESORT AND SPA

The 120-acre resort has canoeing, waterskiing, and two music venues that host performers from the legendary to the up-and-coming. 252 rooms from $89.

8727 Soda Bay Road, Kelseyville | **707/279-4281** | **konoctiharbor.com**

TALLMAN HOTEL

On Upper Lake's Main Street, this 1896 hotel has been tastefully restored and surrounded by new garden cottages. 17 rooms from $109.

9550 Main Street, Upper Lake | **866/708-5253** | **tallmanhotel.com**

SIERRA

THE GOLD CAME FIRST. The wine arrived soon after. Once John Marshall spotted a few shining flakes in the American River at Coloma, the Sierra Foothills filled with miners from around the world. Many came from Chile and France and other places where, unlike the United States, people drank wine. Demand generated supply. By the 1850s, the Lombardo-Fosatti family had started a winery a few miles south of Coloma, and Swiss immigrant Adam Uhlinger had started one in what is now Amador County. There he planted—some believe, anyway—the first Zinfandel vines in California.

The Lombardo-Fosattis' winery is now Boeger Winery, and Uhlinger's winery is still in operation as Sobon Estate. They're proof that in the Sierra Foothills, some roots run deep. But there are new surprises as well. For decades beautiful but sleepy—rolling hills, spreading oaks, 19th-century towns trading off a uniquely compelling past—the area is now increasingly sophisticated. Good restaurants are popping up in unexpected places. Historic towns like Sutter Creek and Murphys draw affluent visitors from San Francisco and Los Angeles. Even more strikingly, an influx of creative new winemakers has made the Sierra Foothills one of the most interesting wine regions in California.

This is a big wine country: The Sierra Foothills AVA extends across eight counties, from Yuba in the north to Calaveras in the south. Within it are smaller appellations, notably El Dorado and Fair Play in El Dorado County and Fiddletown and Shenandoah Valley in Amador County.

Despite its size and geographic diversity, the region for decades was identified with just one wine, Zinfandel. More than a few of the Zin

Continues page 78 >

SUGGESTED ROUTES

☆ **EL DORADO COUNTY** Visit wineries off Carson Road, which runs roughly parallel to Highway 50 between Placerville and Camino

☆ **AMADOR COUNTY** From Plymouth, take Shenandoah Road north to Shenandoah School Road; follow it to Steiner Road then loop back to Plymouth via Shenandoah Road

☆ **CALAVERAS COUNTY** Explore the wineries in Murphys, then head east up Highway 4 to Calaveras Big Trees State Park

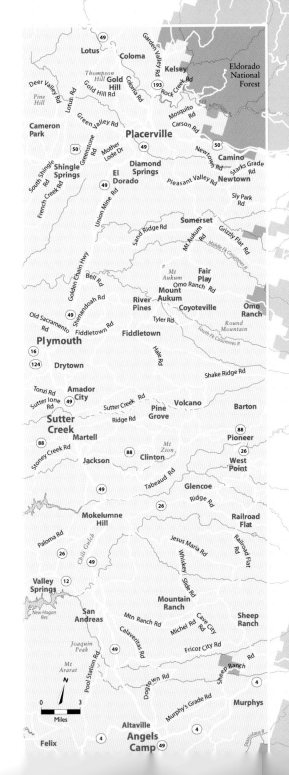

vineyards here are not just old; they're ancient by California standards—planted in the post–Gold Rush years by Adam Uhlinger and other would-be-rich miners forced to return to more traditional ways of making a living from the earth.

The Zinfandel they planted (intertwined with other grapes, we know now) survived in large part because of an enormous customer base who knew very little about true red Zin, but who bought copious amounts of it in the form of sweet white Zinfandel. Sierra Foothills vines catered to this taste and were therefore saved from extinction.

In the last decade or so, the nobler form of the variety has regained a passionate following. And Amador and El Dorado counties especially —with their infamously warm summer days and lesser-known temperature drops at night—are producing some of the state's most intense and powerful versions. Sierra Zins are not for the timid. Their fruit is almost pruny ripe and earthy, with correspondingly high alcohol levels (often pushing past 15 percent). But the best are in balance, with acid and tannins to match. They're spectacular wines. And they've been joined by wines made from Rhône grapes (Syrah, Mourvèdre, Viognier), Italian grapes (Barbera, Sangiovese), and most recently, a Spanish grape (Tempranillo)—all worth watching.

As for wine touring in the Sierra Foothills, it asks that you slow down and enjoy a more relaxed, detour-rich pace. Strung along Highway 49 for nearly 150 miles, the area more or less forces you to choose one appellation to visit per day: El Dorado County, say, then Shenandoah Valley the next day. The expansive, expensive resorts you find in Napa and Sonoma are absent; in their place are historic inns and beds-and-breakfasts, which range from simple to very plush. And the region's wineries, excellent as they've become, have a lot of competition for your attention. No part of California has a richer, more turbulent past: If you're any kind of history buff, for instance, you'll want to visit Marshall Gold Discovery State Historic Park in Coloma. Then there are the natural distractions: hiking beneath the giant sequoias of Calaveras Big Trees State Park, rafting on the South Fork of the American River. They'll give you an adventure or two to toast at the end of the day.

EL DORADO WINERIES

1 | DAVID GIRARD VINEYARDS

The gracious two-story, Tuscan-leaning winery is focused on Rhône-style wines—Syrah, Grenache, Viognier, Roussane. Winemaker Mari Wells has experience at Gloria Ferrer and Pellegrini, where she worked with well-known winemaker Merry Edwards.

741 Cold Springs Road, Placerville | 530/295-1833 | davidgirardvineyards.com

2 | GOLD HILL VINEYARD

Bordeaux varieties were the starting point here, but Italian grapes are coming on strong. Gold Hill brews beer now too—just step over to the bar across the room.

5660 Vineyard Lane, Placerville | 530/626-6522 | goldhillvineyard.com

3 | BOEGER WINERY

Nestled in vineyard blocks planted at different angles, Boeger is a great stop for both history and beauty. A new tasting room stands near the 1870s homestead-winery Greg and Sue Boeger bought in 1972; you can picnic in the pear orchard.

1709 Carson Road, Placerville | 800/655-2634 | boegerwinery.com

4 | MADROÑA VINEYARDS

At about 3,000 feet Madroña can truly lay claim to "mountain Zin." There's a simple, wood-paneled tasting room to try it in, and picnic tables outside under the evergreens.

2560 High Hill Road, Camino | 530/644-5948 | madronavineyards.com

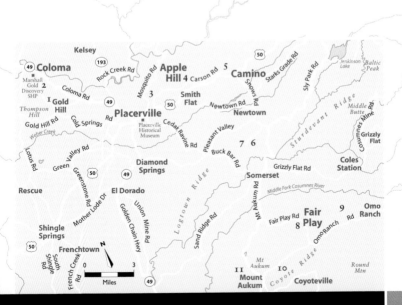

5 | LAVA CAP WINERY

High elevations (2,400 to 2,800 feet) and volcanic soils produce great foothills wines at Lava Cap. Zinfandel is a given, but try the Cabernets too. The redwood deck offers good vineyard views, over territory that was once full of pear orchards.

2221 Fruitridge Road, Placerville | **530/621-0175** | **lavacap.com**

6 | HOLLY'S HILL VINEYARDS

Winemaker Carrie Bendick (Holly's daughter) makes wines that blend European earthiness with mountain fruit. The vineyards, planted to Rhône varieties, are at 2,700 feet, which is why the views behind the tasting room are stunning.

3680 Leisure Lane, Placerville | **530/344-0227** | **hollyshill.com**

7 | SIERRA VISTA VINEYARDS & WINERY

Love of a good view of the Sierra Nevada's Crystal range and interesting Rhône-style wines are enough to bring you here. John and Barbara MacCready were actually ahead of their day in planting Syrah, Grenache, Viognier, and the like in Zinfandel country.

4560 Cabernet Way, Placerville | **800/946-3916** | **sierravistawinery.com**

8 | FITZPATRICK WINERY

The tasting room pairs up with a B&B in a hilltop log lodge at this oldest winery in the Fair Play region. Take advantage of Fitzpatrick's "ploughman's lunch" (until the freshly baked bread runs out) and enjoy the views from the deck.

7740 Fair Play Road, Fair Play | **800/245-9166** | **fitzpatrickwinery.com**

9 | COLIBRI RIDGE WINERY & VINEYARD

You taste right in the working space in this small family winery in the Fair Play AVA, but there's nothing small about the views all around it (bring a picnic).

6100 Gray Rock Road, Fair Play | **530/620-7255** | **colibriridge.com**

10 | LATCHAM VINEYARDS

Winemaker Craig Boyd makes the wines for both the Latcham label and Granite Springs Winery, which is also owned by the Latcham family (5050 Granite Springs Winery Road).

2860 Omo Ranch Road, Mount Aukum | **800/750-5591** | **latcham.com**

11 | C.G. DI ARIE VINEYARD & WINERY

Food scientist Chaim Gur Arieh—who, among other things, helped create Cap'n Crunch cereal—and his artist wife, Elisheva, have built a gorgeous Mediterranean-style wine headquarters. At monthly open houses and by appointment, you can taste their aromatic Shenandoah Valley Zins, tour the art galleries, and take in the rich vistas.

5200 di Arie Road, Mount Aukum | **530/620-6500** | **cgdiarie.com**

THINGS TO DO

APPLE HILL

Vineyards flank the orchards these days. Still, come fall dozens of apple growers offer fresh winesaps and Rome beauties, and pies made from same.

East of Placerville, north of Highway 50 | **530/644-7692** | **applehill.com**

MARSHALL GOLD DISCOVERY STATE HISTORIC PARK

This pretty riverside village is where modern California began.

310 Back Street, Coloma | **530/622-3470** | **parks.ca.gov**

RIVER RAFTING

The South Fork of the American River is one of the most popular rafting runs in the nation. Numerous outfitters offer half-day and day trips from Coloma. Outfitters include **American Whitewater Expeditions** (800/825-3205) and **ARTA River Trips** (800/323-2782); for others, visit coloma.com.

WHERE TO EAT

CAFE LUNA

In downtown Placerville, a shaded retreat for enjoying Italian food and area wines.

451 Main Street, #8, Placerville | **530/642-8669**

GOLD VINE GRILL

In the Fair Play wine district, pastas and steaks and local wines.

6028 Grizzly Flat Road, Somerset | **530/626-4042** | **goldvinegrill.com**

SEQUOIA RESTAURANT

1850s mansion is now one of the most lavish restaurants in the Gold Country.

643 Bee Street, Placerville | **530/622-5222** | **sequoiaplacerville.com**

TOMEI'S

Manhattan supper-club feel in downtown Placerville.

384 Main Street, Placerville | **530/626-9766**

PLACE TO STAY

BEST WESTERN PLACERVILLE INN

Large new motel with pool, Internet access, and more. 105 rooms from $100.

6850 Greenleaf Drive, Placerville | **800/854-9100** | **placervilleinn.com**

AMADOR WINERIES

I | MONTEVINA

This large, monolithic barn—the first winery in Amador County after Prohibition—is built for crowds and known for Zin, but the more interesting varieties are Italian.

20680 Shenandoah School Road, Plymouth | 209/245-6942 | montevina.com

2 | COOPER VINEYARDS

Longtime growers for other wineries, the Coopers are now making a fascinating range of wines in their own pretty stucco winery, from Alicante Bouschet to Primitivo.

21365 Shenandoah School Road, Plymouth | 209/245-6181 | cooperwines.com

3 | SOBON ESTATE

The 150-year-old Sobon Estate is part winery, part museum. But when the best wine being poured in the tasting room is from 100-year-old Zinfandel vines, it's hard to tell where museum breaks off and winery begins.

14430 Shenandoah Road, Plymouth | 209/245-6554 | sobonwine.com

4 | AMADOR FOOTHILL WINERY

You'll find Amador County Zinfandel at its best here. Winemaker Katie Quinn pioneered the idea of single-vineyard Zinfandels in the region, and the great views from the winery's hilltop location make it all the easier to "taste the place" in them.

12500 Steiner Road, Plymouth | 209/245-6307 | amadorfoothill.com

5 | DEAVER VINEYARDS

Some of the Zinfandel vineyards have been here more than 120 years. They were planted by Ken Deaver's grandfather (his great-grandfather had planted Mission grapes here a decade earlier). Cowboy-hatted Deaver recently added Italian varietals.

12455 Steiner Road, Plymouth | 209/245-4099 | deavervineyard.com

6 | SHENANDOAH VINEYARDS

Sister winery to Sobon Estate (they're both organic and owned by the Sobon family), Shenandoah makes a good "ReZerve" Zin and interesting Cabernet Franc.

12300 Steiner Road, Plymouth | 209/245-4455 | sobonwine.com

7 | RENWOOD WINERY

Renwood controls many of the region's Zin vineyards, so its tasting room is a good place to contrast and compare. Grandpère Zin is the signature, but don't discount Grandmère.

12225 Steiner Road, Plymouth | 209/245-6979 | renwood.com

8 | STORY WINERY

In a region of big Zinfandels, Story's might be the heartiest of all. The setting is beautiful, with oak-canopied picnic tables overlooking the Cosumnes River Canyon.

10525 Bell Road, Plymouth | 209/245-6208 | zin.com

9 | DOMAINE DE LA TERRE ROUGE AND EASTON WINES

Two lines of good wines live under one roof here. Terre Rouge is the label for Rhônes (try the beautiful Viognier), while Easton covers Zinfandel and Barbera.

10801 Dickson Road, Plymouth | 209/245-3117 | terrerougewines.com

10 | VINO NOCETO

One of the few wineries in these parts where you can taste multiple versions of Sangiovese, the main grape in Italian Chianti.

11011 Shenandoah Road, Plymouth | 209/245-6556 | noceto.com

THINGS TO DO

DAFFODIL HILL

Near Volcano, the slopes bloom with daffodils from mid-March through mid-April.

**East of Rams Horn Grade, north of Volcano | 209/296-7048 |
amadorcountychamber.com/OnlineVisitorsGuide/FlowerFarms.html**

SUTTER CREEK

Other foothills towns threaten to outgrow their charm. Not Sutter Creek, which remains idyllically shady and walkable.

**On Highway 49, north of Highway 88 | 800/400-0305 |
suttercreek.org**

SUTTER GOLD MINE TOUR

Put on your hardhat and plunge beneath the earth to get a feel for the life of a Sierra miner. Afterwards, attempt to fund your retirement by panning for gold.

Highway 49, Sutter Creek | 866/762-2837 | suttergold.com

WHERE TO EAT

CAFFE VIA D'ORO

A jolt of Italian sophistication in downtown Sutter Creek, Via d'Oro serves steaks and chops and good wine, and live music many nights too.

36 Main Street, Sutter Creek | 209/267-0535

SUTTER CREEK PALACE

Great steaks and local wines in 19th-century setting.

76 Main Street, Sutter Creek | 209/267-1300 | suttercreekpalace.com

TASTE

New, stylish restaurant with ambitious menu and excellent wine list, near Shenandoah Valley wineries.

9402 Main Street, Plymouth | 209/245-3463 | restauranttaste.com

PLACES TO STAY

EUREKA STREET INN

A beautiful arts-and-crafts bungalow was built in 1914 for a stage coach operator —it's been very nicely restored. 4 rooms from $125.

55 Eureka Street, Sutter Creek |800/399-2389 | eurekastreetinn.com

GREY GABLES INN

Britannia rules at this charming inn. 8 rooms from $125.

161 Hanford Street, Sutter Creek | **800/473-9422** | **greygables.com**

THE FOXES INN OF SUTTER CREEK

Beautiful home set behind a long green lawn. 6 rooms from $160.

77 Main Street, Sutter Creek | **209/267-5882** | **foxesinn.com**

THE GATE HOUSE INN

In Jackson, an ornate Victorian home. 3 rooms, 2 suites, and a cottage from $150.

1330 Jackson Gate Road, Jackson | **800/841-1072** | **gatehouseinn.com**

HANFORD HOUSE

Handsome brick inn on the edge of downtown Sutter Creek. 11 rooms from $109.

61 Hanford Street, Sutter Creek | **800/871-5839** | **hanfordhouse.com**

HOTEL LEGER

Balconied hotel, with ghosts, from 1850s boom days. 14 rooms from $55.

8304 Main Street, Mokelumne Hill | **209/286-1401** | **hotelleger.com**

WEDGEWOOD INN

This Wedgewood-blue Victorian home has a carriage house. 5 rooms from $155.

11941 Narcissus Road, Jackson | **800/933/4393** | **wedgewoodinn.com**

SPOTLIGHT DON'T MISS LODI

I t doesn't help that its early wine production ran to sweet Tokay. What did lasting damage was the chorus, sung by Creedence Clearwater Revival in 1969 and reprised by bar bands ever since, "Oh Lord, stuck in Lodi again." But today Lodi, in the San Joaquin Delta south of Sacramento, is one of the most surprising of California's wine regions—worth a stop as you head to the Sierra foothills. Where Tokay once reigned, Zin is now king, often growing on rootstock that dates to the 1800s. Much of Lodi's grapes go to generic California blends, but some become wines that hold their own with Sonoma or Amador county Zins—at half the price. The region has also become much more visitor-friendly, with a **Wine and Visitor Center** *(2545 West Turner Road, Lodi; 209/365-0621; lodiwine.com)* and two dozen wineries open for tasting.*

CALAVERAS WINERIES

1 | STEVENOT WINERY

Barden Stevenot bought this ranch in a tree-filled valley in the 1970s, having been enchanted by visits to the premises as a child. Recently purchased by the Munari family, Stevenot still offers interesting wines under the main label (the Tempranillo, a Spanish grape, is one to watch) in the historic 1870 Shaw Ranch house, and in a tasting room in town, on the corner of Sheep Ranch Road and Main Street.

2690 San Domingo Road, Murphys | 209/728-0638 | stevenotwinery.com

2 | ZUCCA MOUNTAIN VINEYARDS

Try Sangiovese with chocolate fondue in Zucca Mountain's grottolike tasting room under a 150-year-old building across from the Murphys Hotel. This small family operation produces Zinfandel along with Italian wines, and even blends the two.

425 Main Street, Murphys | 209/728-1623 | zuccawines.com

3 | NEWSOME-HARLOW VINEYARDS

The small, handsome Newsome-Harlow tasting room—and the Bordeaux blend, Zinfandel, Cabernet Sauvignon Blanc, and Sauvignon Blanc poured here—are a partnership between grower Mark Skenfield, winemaker Scott Klann (both locally grown themselves), and attorney Hugh Swift. Resident chef Melanie Klann is adept at fashioning recipes that set off the wines well.

403 Main Street, Murphys | 209/728-9817 | newsome-harlow.com

4 | MILLIAIRE WINERY

Steve Miller, who directs all the winemaking at Ironstone, satisfies his need to make higher-end wine in an old Flying A gas station on Main Street. The contrast between the wines and space here and those at Ironstone says much about winemaking in the region. Try his version of Zinfandel from the Clockspring Vineyard.

276 Main Street, Murphys | 209/728-1658 | milliairewinery.com

5 | IRONSTONE VINEYARDS

Nothing short of an institution, Ironstone makes about 300,000 cases of wine a year and draws some 500,000 visitors to its gardens, caves, museum (containing the largest crystalline gold piece in the world), stamp mill where kids can learn mining techniques, and outdoor concert venue. While most of its wines are designed for mass appeal, the Cabernet Franc is quite interesting.

1894 Six Mile Road, Murphys | 209/728-1251 | ironstonevineyards.com

6 | CHATOM VINEYARDS

Its location on the main highway makes it a convenient stop, which means you won't be alone when you visit. The Semillon here is worth a try.

1969 Highway 4, Douglas Flat | 209/736-6500 | chatomvineyards.com

7 | IRISH VINEYARDS

There's beautiful countryside around the 1867 Batten farmhouse the Irish family bought to found a winery on, and a lot of Irish spirit layered on the mind-boggling number of wines they make here, from sparkling to Malvasia Bianca to apricot wine. The Chenin Blanc and Petite Sirah are promising.

2849 Highway 4, Vallecito | 209/736-1299 | irishvineyard.com

8 | TWISTED OAK WINERY

Everything is twisted here—the road going up, the humor on signs and labels ("@#$," reads one; "Ask for the wine by name," demands co-owner Jeff Stai), and the grand oak at the top of the hill—to say nothing of the vast number of rubber chickens on display. But the Rhône- and Spanish-style wines are serious, and also available at the winery's second tasting room in Murphys (350 Main Street). Twisted Oak answers the question, What would it be like if Monty Python made good wine?

4280 Red Hill Road, Vallecito | 209/736-9080 | twistedoak.com

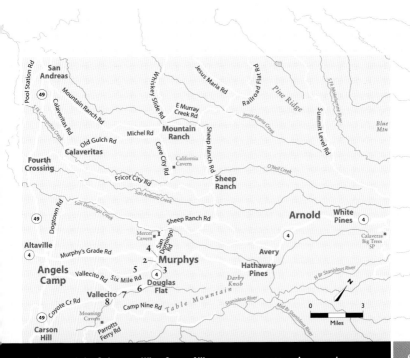

THINGS TO DO

CALAVERAS BIG TREES STATE PARK

Magnificent stands of giant sequoias were among the first of their species to be discovered in California and are still guaranteed to awe.

State Highway 4, 4 miles east of Arnold | 209/795-2334 | parks.ca.gov

RAILTOWN 1897 STATE HISTORIC PARK

Just south of the Calaveras/Tuolumne County line, this historic park commemorates the Sierra Railway, which started here in 1897 and carried passengers throughout the Gold Country. In modern times, the trains have gone Hollywood: parts of *High Noon* were filmed here, and *Back to the Future 3*. Visit and you can see train exhibits and, April through October, ride the rails yourself.

5th Avenue and Reservoir Road, Jamestown | 209/984-3953 | railtown1897.org

SPELUNKING

The Sierra foothills are California's capital of caves, with three notable caverns in Calaveras County alone: **Mercer Caverns** (Sheep Ranch Road, Murphys; 209/728-2101; mercercaverns.com); **California Cavern** (9565 Cave City Road, Mountain Ranch; 209/736-2708; caverntours.com); and **Moaning Cavern** (Moaning Cave Road off Parrotts Ferry Road, Vallecito; 209/736-2708; caverntours.com). All are open for tours. At Moaning you descend via 100-foot spiral staircase or 165-foot-rope rappel, so we suggest saving the wine tasting for afterwards.

SPOTLIGHT ERNA'S ELDERBERRY HOUSE

I t's all the way in Oakhurst, near the southern entrance to Yosemite National Park and an hour south of the Sierra wine country. But food- and wine-lovers happily make the pilgrimage to Erna's Elderberry House and Chateau Sureau (48688 Victoria Lane, Oakhurst; 559/683-8600; elderberryhouse.com). ☆ Austrian-born Erna Kubin-Clanin opened the restaurant in 1984 and quickly garnered raves for her six-course, prix-fixe California-French dinners and her wine list. In the 1990s she added the 10-room Chateau Sureau, a place Marie Antoinette would have loved had she ever visited Madera County. For the choosy guest, there's Villa Sureau. The rates for these pleasures? Around $90 for dinner (not including wine), $500 for a room, $2,800 for the villa.

WHERE TO EAT

ALCHEMY MARKET AND WINE BAR

Great soups and sandwiches, nice selection of local wines.

191 Main Street, Murphys | 209/728-0700 | alchemymarket.com

FIREWOOD

Wood-fired pizzas that demand accompaniment by a fierce Sierra foothill Zin.

420 Main Street, Murphys | 209/728-3248

MURPHYS GRILLE

Good steaks, local wines, nice porchside view of downtown Murphys.

380 Main Street, #1, Murphys | 209/728-8800

V RESTAURANT AND BAR

Ambitious, Mediterranean-influenced cuisine in the Gold Country.

402 Main Street, Murphys | 209/728-0107

PLACES TO STAY

ARNOLD BLACK BEAR INN

At 4,000 feet, this rustic but luxurious timber-framed inn sits among pine forests northeast of Murphys. Enjoy the outdoor spa under the trees. 5 rooms from $185.

1343 Oak Circle, Arnold | 209/795-8999 | blackbearinn.com

DUNBAR HOUSE

Stay in a beautiful home near a creek. 5 rooms from $175.

271 Jones Street, Murphys | 209/728-2897 | dunbarhouse.com

MURPHYS HOTEL

Venerable hotel offers shared-bath rooms and newer units. 29 rooms from $59.

457 Main Street, Murphys | 800/532-7684 | murphyshotel.com

QUERENCIA

One-of-a-kind inn on hilltop above town. 4 rooms from $275, breakfast included.

4383 Sheep Ranch Road, Murphys | 209/728-9520 | querencia.ws

VICTORIA INN

A modern inn that sits nicely in downtown Murphys. 14 rooms from $115.

402 Main Street, Murphys | 209/728-8933 | victoriainn-murphys.com

SANTA CRUZ

THE SANTA CRUZ MOUNTAINS are the San Francisco Bay Area's backyard wine country. Look on a map and you see that many of the region's wineries lie only 10 or 20 miles from the office parks and affluent suburbs of the San Francisco Peninsula and greater San Jose.

But that geography is misleading. Once you're in the Santa Cruz Mountains—once you've driven the twisting roads that invariably take longer than you expected from looking at the map—you're in a land that is wilder than you could have imagined, where sunlight filters through old-growth redwoods and the turns in the road reveal surprising views of the sea. Winemaking here is also a bit wild, with larger-than-life characters towering over the local scene like those redwoods and wines that are as surprising as the views.

The Santa Cruz Mountains AVA extends across 400,000 acres in three counties—Santa Cruz, Santa Clara, and San Mateo—but only 1,500 acres of the AVA are actually planted in grapes. The topography ranges from sun-splashed (and, alternately, fog-shrouded) meadows overlooking the ocean to deep, redwood-shaded canyons to drier hills. Running through the middle of things is the San Andreas Fault: the 1989 Loma Prieta quake was centered here. Demographically the region is just as varied. Its eastern gateways are three of Silicon Valley's toniest suburbs: Los Gatos, Saratoga, and Woodside, towns where dot-com bazillionaires plan state-of-the-art wine cellars knowing they'll be able to stock them with superb Thomas Fogarty or Ridge bottles from just up the hill. (Many of these new estates have their own acre-or-so vineyards.) To the south is Santa Cruz, which, despite a recent high-tech influx, remains its unique self: part college town, part surf town, home to impassioned political dissent but always happy to kick back with a nice glass of local Pinot. In between are the redwood villages of Felton and Boulder Creek. Stretching to the west is the Pacific coast—not as dramatic here as at Big Sur, but quietly, deeply beautiful.

One of the first AVAs in America to be defined by terrain, the Santa Cruz Mountains has as long a wine-growing history as any region in the state. After logging cleared much of the land of redwoods in the mid-1800s, many vines were planted. They suffered the same setbacks—Prohibition, the Depression, and phylloxera—as their counterparts elsewhere, as well as a huge fire.

The winemakers who were drawn here after World War II were (and still are) of a kind, really. There's a little more isolation and a little less convention in these hills than in most other California wine regions, inviting original characters and iconoclasts; a few have made the place what it is today. Famously opinionated Martin Ray bought the old Paul Masson winery before selling it to Seagram & Sons (the historic property is now the Mountain Winery, a popular music venue in the summer). Ray went on to found Mount Eden Vineyards, whose Chardonnay shows what Santa Cruz Mountains wineries are capable of.

Randall Grahm of Bonny Doon stretches even the Santa Cruz definition of originality. A former grad student in philosophy at UC Santa Cruz, he has built one of the state's most enormous small wineries (the former being the reality; the latter, the perception) with the goal of making the world unsafe for Chardonnay and Cabernet. He has ridden with the Rhône Rangers, bottled countless obscure varietals, buried the inventor of corks with public funerals and a commitment to screw caps, and consistently impressed critics with his core Rhône blend, "Le Cigare Volant" (The Flying Cigar). Naturally the tasting room is as rustic as the mountains, and one of the staff will pull out an aboriginal didgeridoo and blow some excruciating blasts in celebration if you join the Bonny Doon wine club.

None of these Santa Cruz Mountains visionaries has made as big a mark on the international wine world, though, as Paul Draper of Ridge Vineyards, widely considered the dean of California winemaking. In the

Continues page 93 >

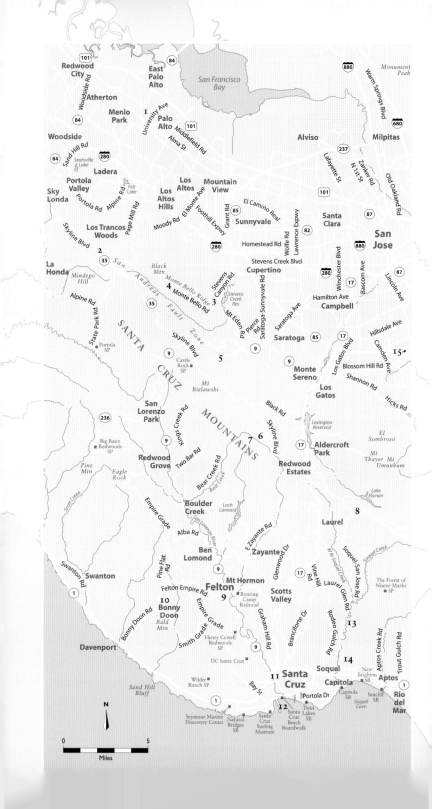

now-famous 2006 rematch of the 1976 Judgment of Paris tasting, in which California Cabernets bested the Bordeaux (much to the chagrin of the predominantly French tasters on the panel), the same Ridge Monte Bello Cab won over the entire field (it came in fifth 30 years ago). More than one wine writer has slipped and reported that, once again, Napa Cabs have proved they're every bit as good—and long-lived—as Bordeaux. But no, number one would be a Santa Cruz Mountains Cab.

Clearly, a substantial contingent of makers has been producing great wines all along in these mountains (although most produce wines from other places too; there are precious few vineyards here to serve all needs). Others are just getting started. Individualists all, they're not eager to hire high-powered wine consultants or follow beaten paths. If there's a dearth of familiar elegance in their wines due to this unwillingness to follow conventions, there's also a range of personality that more than fills the gap. Santa Cruz Mountains wines are interesting—full of the complexities that stony soils, mountain elevations, and fog-driven hang time induce.

And because of its proximity to the Bay Area, the Santa Cruz Mountains is an easy place for a weekend or a day of wine tasting. The wineries on its eastern side can readily be reached from San Jose and

Continues page 94 >

SUGGESTED ROUTES

☆ **SKYLINE BOULEVARD (STATE 35)** *Starting at Skyline's intersection with Highway 84 in Woodside and continuing south for 30 occasionally winding miles, this is one of the great drives in California, giving you views of San Francisco Bay to the east and of folded green mountains and ocean to the west. It also leads to some of the area's best wineries: Thomas Fogarty and David Bruce (both just off Skyline), and Burrell School.*

☆ **HIGHWAY 1** *From Davenport south, you parallel the Pacific, then head inland a couple of miles to hit the tasting room at Bonny Doon Vineyard. Double back and continue south to the wineries and wine bars of Santa Cruz.*

☆ **SOQUEL** *For an easy half-day of wine tasting, exit off Highway 17 to Soquel's Main Street, then turn right on Glen Haven. You'll catch three wineries and numerous antiques stores.*

the San Francisco Peninsula, those on the west side reached from Santa Cruz. That said, wine touring here is different than in Napa or Sonoma. There are fewer wineries, and greater distances between them—and the winding roads make that distance seem longer. With the exception of a few—Byington, David Bruce, Fogarty—most of the tasting rooms are cozy rather than grand. (A good number are only open on weekends, so check before you set out.) Even so, you may find that these mountains, and their wines, end up occupying a special place in your heart. From the porch at Bonny Doon Vineyard, for instance, you can sip an estimable Rhône blend, gaze out at redwoods, and feel the breeze stirring from the Pacific a few miles down the hill. The world, with its troubles, will feel far, far away.

SANTA CRUZ WINERIES

1 | VINO LOCALE

Located across the street from Zibibbo in downtown Palo Alto, Vino Locale is a charming little cafe that also sells local wines, many from Santa Cruz Mountains wineries that lack tasting rooms of their own.

431 Kipling Street, Palo Alto | 650/328-0450 | vinolocale.com

2 | THOMAS FOGARTY WINERY

In a glorious spot on Skyline Boulevard overlooking the whole of Silicon Valley, Thomas Fogarty is one of the few "uptown" Santa Cruz Mountains wineries—its namesake founder is a heart surgeon who invented a still-widely used medical device. While some of Fogarty's best known wines aren't grown in the region (including its Gewürztraminer, a popular go-to partner for Thai food), the estate Chardonnays and Pinot Noirs are.

19501 Skyline Boulevard, Woodside | 650/851-6777 | fogartywinery.com

3 | PICCHETTI WINERY

A very short drive from civilization (just east of Ridge), Picchetti represents another piece of California winemaking history. The Picchetti brothers built the place in 1896 (it's on the National Registry of Historic Places), had to forsake winemaking for general ranching during Prohibition, and finally sold their holdings in the 1960s. Leslie Pantling has put the wine back in these ranch buildings, and is even working a few acres of 100-plus-year-old Zinfandel vines. Picnic tables are available, if you don't mind the peacocks.

13100 Monte Bello Road, Cupertino | 408/741-1310 | picchetti.com

4 | RIDGE VINEYARDS

This is the home of the Cabernet that beat out France's top Bordeaux—again—in the 2006 rematch of the 1976 Judgment of Paris tasting. Paul Draper has been at the winemaking helm since 1969, advocating balance as opposed to huge fruit and alcohol levels. The winery's Lytton Springs tasting room, in the heart of Sonoma Zinfandel land, might be newer and cooler, but the Monte Bello facility is adjacent to what's arguably the best Cabernet vineyard in the world.

17100 Monte Bello Road, Cupertino | 408/867-3233 | ridgewine.com

5 | SAVANNAH-CHANELLE VINEYARDS

Tasting at the roomy, barnlike Savannah-Chanelle is an opportunity to compare Pinot Noirs from many of the major Pinot regions in the state—the Russian River Valley, the Sonoma Coast, Arroyo Grande—as well as the estate around you. Located just above the town of Saratoga, it's an easy afternoon stop.

23600 Big Basin Way, Saratoga | 408/741-2934 | savannahchanelle.com

6 | DAVID BRUCE WINERY

When many wine lovers think of Santa Cruz Mountains Pinot Noir, they think of David Bruce. One of the pioneers here, Bruce founded his concrete winery in the trees in 1964 and now makes in the neighborhood of 60,000 cases a year. While his reputation rides on Pinot, he has always played with other grapes; try the Petite Sirah.

21439 Bear Creek Road, Los Gatos | 800/397-9972 | davidbrucewinery.com

SPOTLIGHT LIVERMORE VALLEY

Just north and east of the Santa Cruz Mountains is the San Francisco Bay Area's other wine region, the Livermore Valley. The first commercial vineyards were planted here in the 1840s, and the valley's two most acclaimed wineries, Wente Vineyards and Concannon Vineyard, each got its start in 1883. Today, thanks to an agreement that limits housing growth, the valley boasts several dozen wineries. At one end of the spectrum is tiny **Cedar Mountain** (7000 Tesla Road; 925/373-6636; wines.com/cedarmountain), which produces both a Cabernet and a Chardonnay from fruit grown in its 14-acre Blanches Vineyard. At the other end is giant **Wente** (5565 Tesla Road; 925/456-2405; wentevineyards.com), with its own golf course, restaurant, and even a summer concert series. For more about Livermore Valley wines, visit livermorewine.com or call 925/447-9463.

7 | BYINGTON VINEYARD & WINERY

Up winding Bear Creek Road, Byington is worth visiting for the beauty of the place alone. Like most of the other larger producers here, Byington makes many of its wines from grapes grown outside the mountains, including an interesting dry rosé, which they were bottling long before it was all the rage.

21850 Bear Creek Road, Los Gatos | 408/354-1111 | byington.com

8 | BURRELL SCHOOL VINEYARDS & WINERY

It took Anne and David Moulton a few years to quit their day jobs in Silicon Valley and move up to this historic 1854 schoolhouse they had bought and surrounded with vineyards. Unlike many local vintners, the Moultons only make Santa Cruz Mountains–derived wines. The school theme runs throughout: The best wine is "Valedictorian." Don't miss the crisp and minerally Chardonnay and the Cabernet Franc.

24060 Summit Road, Los Gatos | 408/353-6290 | burrellschool.com

9 | HALLCREST VINEYARDS

Today's Hallcrest, in the little town of Felton, is the rebirth of a 1940s winery that helped put the Santa Cruz Mountains on the winemaking map. The tasting room is quaint, casual, and a little cluttered—there are also a couple of lovely spots for picnickers.

379 Felton Empire Road, Felton | 831/335-4441 | hallcrestvineyards.com

10 | BONNY DOON VINEYARD

The staff in this rustic retreat channels the refreshing lunacy and the complete lack of wine pretension of owner Randall Grahm. Diverse is an understatement when applied to Bonny Doon wines: The wild lineup is infinitely interesting, often eccentric, usually yummy, and at its best, grand. The label art alone will hold your interest. Bring a picnic for lunch out back by beautiful Mill Creek.

10 Pine Flat Road, Santa Cruz | 831/425-4518 | bonnydoonvineyard.com

11 | STORRS WINERY

This industrial park tasting room is a good place to try wines from a number of tucked-away places in the mountains, such as the Christie Vineyard Chardonnay.

Old Sash Mill, 303 Potrero Street, # 35, Santa Cruz | 831/458-5030 | storrswine.com

12 | BEAUREGARD VINEYARDS

Visit Beauregard's tasting room right on the wharf. Four generations have grown grapes in the nearby mountains; the last two are finally making them into wine, and are perhaps the only winemakers to champion the tiny Ben Lomond AVA on their bottles.

55B Municipal Wharf, Santa Cruz | 831/425-7777 | beauregardvineyards.com

1 3 | SOQUEL VINEYARDS

One of the newest winery facilities in the hills above Santa Cruz, Soquel is linked to local family history: Two of its owners are Peter and Paul Bargetto of the Bargetto winery family, and its redwood doors are made from a 12,000-gallon tank their grandfather bought in the 1940s. While the Bargetto twins (along with partner Jon Morgan) have a vineyard in the works, their grapes are still primarily sourced from other places, including Napa and the Russian River Valley.

8063 Glen Haven Road, Soquel | 831/462-9045 | soquelvineyards.com

1 4 | BARGETTO WINERY

The Bargettos go way back—brothers Phillip and John bought their property in 1918. The third generation is in charge now. And while this tasting room tucked in a pictur-esque spot by a creek has been known for its interesting fruit wines (and a slightly eccentric mead), the focus has shifted to core Santa Cruz Mountains wine. Bargetto's Regan Estate Vineyards, for example, is a 40-acre plot that sits on a knoll overlooking Monterey Bay. The Chardonnay grapes that grow there like the cool climate.

3535 North Main Street, Soquel | 831/475-2258, ext. 14 | bargetto.com

1 5 | CLOS LA CHANCE WINES

For a huge change of pace from cozy mountain tasting rooms, drive south on Highway 101 to San Martin and Clos La Chance. Technically outside the AVA, Clos La Chance makes quite a bit of Santa Cruz Mountains wine. In fact, owners Bill and Brenda Murphy got into the business with a backyard vineyard at their house in Saratoga. Here, they throw all the high-tech bells and whistles at winegrowing and making, which makes for lively tours. Everything about this place is grand: tasting room, terrace, lawn, views. Bring a picnic or order one ahead of time; you can even get in some bocce ball or taste with your kids (they get sparkling cider).

1 Hummingbird Lane, San Martin | 408/686-1050 | closlachance.com

FAVORITES & DISCOVERIES ☆ SANTA CRUZ

RIDGE VINEYARDS *The best wine in the world is made from grapes grown in the Santa Cruz Mountains winery's Monte Bello vineyard*

DAVID BRUCE WINERY *Pinot Noir has been the winery's passion since its founding in the 1960s*

BONNY DOON VINEYARD *The labels on its bottles and the antics of its founder may get lots of press, but the wine delivers the goods*

BURRELL SCHOOL VINEYARDS & WINERY *Views from the wrap-around deck are worth writing a double-spaced essay about*

THINGS TO DO

BIG BASIN STATE PARK

This 18,000-acre shrine to the coast redwood is the oldest state park in California, and one of the best: There are few easier, or prettier, places to see the tall trees. Camp or stay in a tent cabin. You can access the park from Highway 236 or from Highway 1 north of Santa Cruz.

21600 Big Basin Way, Boulder Creek | 831/338-8860 | bigbasin.org

CAPITOLA AND SOQUEL

Capitola is just what a California beach town should be: compact, walkable, blessed with a summery sense of history (some of its wooden cottages date from its days as a 19th-century resort), but still a good place for teens to show off tans and tattoos. Adjacent Soquel has a pleasing Main Street and three wineries.

**Capitola-Soquel Chamber of Commerce |
716-G Capitola Avenue, Capitola | 831/475-6522 | capitolachamber.com**

MIDPENINSULA REGIONAL OPEN SPACE DISTRICT

In between Skyline Boulevard's wineries, you'll notice signs for preserves managed by this nonprofit conservation group: Windy Hill, Russian Ridge, and more. They're all beautiful, all are worth exploring, and many have good picnic areas.

650/691-1200 | openspace.org

NATURAL BRIDGES STATE BEACH

On the northern edge of Santa Cruz, this coast-hugging state park is famous for its tidepools and rocky coves and the swarms of monarch butterflies that gather in its eucalyptus groves in early winter.

**2531 West Cliff Drive, Santa Cruz | 831/423-4609 |
santacruzstateparks.org**

ROARING CAMP RAILROADS

Tourists have choo-choo'ed through the redwoods here since 1875. Today, Roaring Camp offers steam-train excursions through the trees as well as trips to and from the Santa Cruz Beach Boardwalk.

Felton | 831/335-4484 | roaringcamp.com

SANTA CRUZ BEACH BOARDWALK

When considering what wine to pair with a corn dog and a spin on the Giant Dipper, you want an assertive red that—no, forget it. The Beach Boardwalk has nothing to do with wine. Nevertheless, this beachside fun zone is one of the classic amusement parks in the nation—and that 80-year-old wooden Giant

Dipper roller coaster one of the best in the world. Eminently worth visiting if you're wine-touring in the Santa Cruz area, especially if you have children in tow.

400 Beach Street, Santa Cruz | 831/423-5590 | beachboardwalk.com

SANTA CRUZ, DOWNTOWN

The city's heart, Pacific Avenue, has waxed and waned over the years. It got badly whacked by the 1989 Loma Prieta earthquake but is now enjoying a genuine renaissance, its handsome buildings holding all sorts of college-town fun: movie theaters, good bookstores, funky/chic clothing stores, a bevy of restaurants, and enough coffee spots to launch a thousand term papers.

Pacific Avenue, Santa Cruz | 831/429-8433 | downtownsantacruz.com

SEYMOUR MARINE DISCOVERY CENTER AT LONG MARINE LAB

Run by UC Santa Cruz, this friendly facility is great fun for the kids and a fine place to discover the wonders of the Pacific.

100 Shaffer Road, Santa Cruz | 831/459-3800 | www2.ucsc.edu/seymourcenter

SHAKESPEARE SANTA CRUZ

If you're visiting July through September you can't go wrong by attending one of this award-laden regional theater company's performances. Those held in the redwood forest–wrapped outdoor amphitheater are especially magical.

1156 High Street, Santa Cruz | 831/459-2159 | shakespearesantacruz.org

SURFING

Santa Cruz has been wrestling with Huntington Beach for the title of Surf City USA for a decade. We're not going to get into that imbroglio: Suffice to say this is a great place for novices to learn to surf, thanks to the lessons given by wave gurus Richard Schmidt (Richard Schmidt Surf School; 831/423-0928; richardschmidt.com) and Ed Guzman (Club Ed Surf School; 831/464-0177; club-ed.com). And the city's surf museum, housed in the Mark Abbott Memorial Lighthouse above surf mecca Steamer Lane, is sweetly rad (701 West Cliff Drive; 831/420-6289; santacruzsurfingmuseum.org).

WILDER RANCH STATE PARK

A former dairy farm on the coast north of Santa Cruz, Wilder Ranch now offers great hiking and mountain biking on 34 miles of trails, not to mention glorious ocean views.

1401 Old Coast Road, Santa Cruz | 831/423-9703 | santacruzstateparks.org

WHERE TO EAT

GABRIELLA CAFE

Sunset has dubbed this the most romantic spot to dine in Santa Cruz, and we stand by the judgment. The setting (a cozy yellow cottage), the food (lovely salads, pastas, fish), and the wine all make this a great spot for a date, be it your first or your 500th.

910 Cedar Street, Santa Cruz | 831/457-1677 | gabriellacafe.com

GAYLE'S BAKERY AND ROSTICCERIA

On any weekend you'll see crowds lining up at this Capitola favorite, and for good reason. Sandwiches, pastas, and entrées (for takeout or to eat here) and phenomenal breads, pastries, and cakes—everything Gayle's makes is wonderful.

504 Bay Avenue, Capitola | 831/462-1200 | gaylesbakery.com

MANRESA

Chef David Kinch's restaurant vaulted Los Gatos from mere affluent Silicon Valley suburb to gourmet destination, as foodies (and food magazines) from around the world heaped praise on a menu that draws inspiration from France and Catalonia and its ingredients from the Santa Cruz Mountains.

320 Village Lane, Los Gatos | 408/354-4330 | manresarestaurant.com

OSWALD

With sophisticated, exquisitely prepared food and an ambitious wine list, Oswald raised the bar for Santa Cruz dining when it opened a couple of years ago. At our press time, it was slated to move from its current Pacific Avenue location to another downtown venue. Give them a call and track the new address down—you won't be sorry.

1547 Pacific Avenue, Santa Cruz | 831/423-7427

PEARL ALLEY BISTRO

The bistro has been in Santa Cruz for what seems like forever, but don't take it for granted. The menu, which changes seasonally but draws continued inspiration from local produce, is as adventuresome as it is appealing, and the intimate setting is a charmer.

110 Pearl Alley, Santa Cruz | 831/429-8070 | pearlalley.com

SHADOWBROOK

This elegant restaurant is famous for three things: a hillside/creekside location so dramatic you arrive via funicular railway; a savvy way with steak and fresh fish; and a phenomenal wine list (including numerous Santa Cruz Mountains vintages).

1750 Wharf Road, Capitola | **831/475-1511** | **shadowbrook-capitola.com**

SOIF WINE BAR

Just what downtown Santa Cruz needed: a chic wine bar with a great selection of wines and tasty tapas. The adjoining wine shop has good offerings, too, including some otherwise hard-to-find local vintages.

105 Walnut Avenue, Santa Cruz | **831/423-2020** | **soifwine.com**

PLACES TO STAY

BABBLING BROOK BED AND BREAKFAST INN

Very Santa Cruz: beneath the redwood trees, a nest of brown-shingled cottages tidily arranged alongside the promised babbling brook, with lots of hidden decks and patios to relax on. Surprisingly, all this verdure is located on the edge of downtown, which makes for some traffic noise but easy access to good restaurants. 13 rooms from $145.

1025 Laurel Street, Santa Cruz | **831/427-2437** |
innsbythesea.com/babbling-brook

COSTANOA

If your spouse has never liked camping, take him/her here. On the coast 30 minutes north of Santa Cruz, this unique resort has elegant tent cabins that can make a camping convert out of almost anybody—there are indoor rooms for die-hard urbanites. The Cascade restaurant, plus the wine and food offerings at Costanoa's General Store, will help, too, as will the spa treatments. 172 lodge rooms, tent cabins, and shared cabins from $95.

2001 Rossi Road, Pescadero | **650/879-1100** | **costanoa.com**

HOTEL LOS GATOS

A pleasing hotel in the middle of a very appealing town. 72 rooms from $313.

210 East Main Street, Los Gatos | **408/335-1700** | **hotellosgatos.com**

INN AT DEPOT HILL

In Capitola, convenient to the beach and the wineries of nearby Soquel, this 1881 railroad depot that's been converted into a swank inn is one of the best B&Bs anywhere. All rooms are elegantly themed: the Portofino, the Kyoto, and so on. Wonderful breakfasts, too. 12 rooms from $180.

250 Monterey Avenue, Capitola | **800/572-2632** |
innsbythesea.com/depot-hill

M O N T E R E Y

"TWO GALLONS IS A GREAT DEAL OF WINE, *even for two paisanos. Spiritually the jugs may be graduated thus: Just below the shoulder of the first bottle, serious and concentrated conversation. Two inches farther down, sweetly sad memory. Three inches more, thoughts of old and satisfactory loves."*

—JOHN STEINBECK, *Tortilla Flat*

A lot of things have changed since John Steinbeck described winetasting in the raffish Monterey of the 1920s. The region's wines have risen from the cheap jug variety to some of California's great ones. But some things haven't altered—notably the deep, almost sensual links between Monterey County wines and the sculpted valleys and hills from which they spring.

It seems almost unfair that Monterey County should produce high-quality wines. It already has, in Point Lobos and Big Sur, the most stunningly gorgeous coast in the world, and in Pebble Beach the most stunningly affluent. It has Carmel's carefully rustic charm. It has marine science in the Monterey Bay Aquarium and fine art in Steinbeck's novels and Robinson Jeffers' poems. It has artichokes and world-class golf. Why does it even need grapes?

But grapes it has. In terms of serious winemaking (as opposed to *Tortilla Flat*'s backyard version), this is a young region. High above Soledad, on the east side of the fertile Salinas Valley, Chalone Vineyard traces its history back to the 1920s. With this exception, large-scale production dates only from the 1970s, when pioneers like Jerry Lohr began planting grapes in the valley. Today Monterey County is a wine powerhouse, with 40,000 acres of vineyards planted in eight appellations that range from sprawling Monterey to Hames Valley and tiny Chalone.

While AVAs everywhere in California tend to be complicated wheels within wheels, in Monterey County they are especially confounding. The official Monterey appellation doesn't comprise the whole county, and in fact, some of the smaller AVAs—Carmel Valley, Hames Valley— fall outside of it. More surprising is that most of the best wine (most of the worst too, for that matter) doesn't come from near the well-known destinations by the bay but from the length of the Salinas Valley east of the Santa Lucia Range.

Here, the wind has legendary strength on summer afternoons (reportedly starting at 2 PM), pulling in an ocean chill from the north. Early in its wine history, the flat Salinas Valley floor offered a cooler rival to the San Joaquin Valley for slightly better-quality bulk wine, which it still delivers in spades today. But at the fine-wine level, mistakes were made. Cabernet Sauvignon—the main red wine of choice in those days— was widely planted throughout, but the north valley was just too cold for it. Monterey Cabs got a bad rap for their "veggie" qualities.

Growers have been sorting things out and replanting, though, putting cool-weather lovers like Pinot Noir and Chardonnay in the north valley and grapes with warmer needs to the south. Along the way, a handful of very special regions has emerged. One of the most exciting is a narrow strip of benchland on the west side of the Salinas Valley: the Santa Lucia Highlands, put on the map by maverick grower—and now winemaker— Gary Pisoni of Pisoni Vineyards and Winery. A Pisoni Pinot is a thing of intense beauty, and very hard to come by. Fortunately, Pisoni's neighbors are following suit. Directly across the valley, up in the Gabilan Range, the Chalone AVA produces distinctive Chardonnays, full of fruit and the limestone-rich soil they're grown in. It's well worth breaking up a drive down the 101 corridor for a jog to the west or east to take a sip or two.

Touring Monterey's wine country is not like touring other California wine regions. Many of the best wineries—like Gary Pisoni's in the Santa Lucia Highlands and Michaud in Chalone—are not open to the public. And some of the most visitor-friendly stops are really only tasting rooms

Continues page 105 >

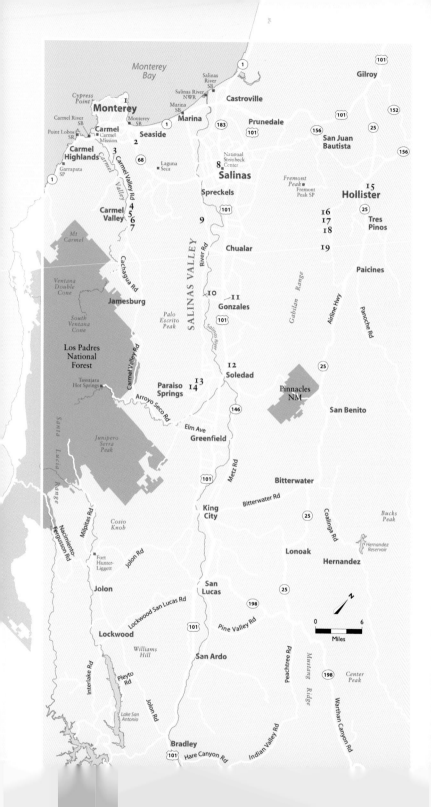

for wineries elsewhere (this practice is common in Carmel Valley). That said, no place makes it easier to add wine tasting to a vacation. Carmel Valley's wineries are a short side trip from Carmel-by-the-Sea. The Taste of Monterey tasting room is a five-minute walk from the Monterey Bay Aquarium, while its Salinas sibling is next door to the Steinbeck Museum. For a longer tour, drive south from Salinas along River Road, through the Santa Lucia Highlands: It's the new classic California, where vineyards are interspersed with lettuce and broccoli fields.

Due east of Monterey County, San Benito County is California's stealth wine region—respected by winemakers, little known by the public. But this, too, is a beautiful pocket of California. With its graceful mission and its sense of keeping one foot firmly in the 19th century, San Juan Bautista is one of the most appealing towns in California. From here, State Highway 25—lonely but glorious, especially in spring—hopscotches the San Andreas Fault as it runs south into the Gabilan Mountains. Josh Jensen's Calera Wine Company is the standout here: From vineyards very close to the Chalone AVA, but on the east side of the mountains, Jensen makes different single-vineyard Pinot Noirs that take advantage of that limestone soil and set standards for the variety. Newer comers to the county, such as Léal Vineyards, with bottlings from Chardonnay and Sauvignon Blanc to Bordeaux varieties and blends, are making San Benito a region to watch.

SUGGESTED ROUTES

☆ **CARMEL VALLEY ROAD** *A pretty (if sometimes busy) drive that takes you to a half-dozen tasting rooms, a number of good nurseries, and some of the region's poshest resorts*

☆ **RIVER ROAD** *Starting near Salinas and running along the west side of the Salinas Valley to Greenfield, River Road leads to a half-dozen wineries*

☆ **HIGHWAY 25** *History, scenery and a few choice wineries between San Juan Bautista and Pinnacles National Monument*

MONTEREY WINERIES

1 | TASTE OF MONTEREY

This Cannery Row facility—with great bay views—offers a terrific rotating selection of county wines for tasting and for sale, including many from wineries not normally open to the public. You can buy a glass and settle in by the bank of otter-view windows.

700 Cannery Row, Monterey | 831/646-5446 | tasteofmonterey.com

2 | VENTANA VINEYARDS

With a tasting room just a few miles east of downtown, this is an easy winery to visit. The wines come from owner Doug Meador's vineyards on the west side of the Salinas Valley.

2999 Monterey-Salinas Highway, Monterey | 831/372-7415 | ventanawines.com

3 | CHÂTEAU JULIEN WINE ESTATE

The château is a showstopper on the beautiful road winding up to the Village, and the patio out back makes a good picnic stop. Try the Sangiovese.

8940 Carmel Valley Road, Carmel | 831/624-2600 | chateaujulien.com

4 | HELLER ESTATE

The stucco tasting room might be heavy on the wine goods, but you can stroll through the sculpture garden and taste organic wines. The Chardonnays are noteworthy.

69 West Carmel Valley Road, Carmel Valley | 831/659-6220 | hellerestate.com

5 | GEORIS

Merlot stars for Walter Georis, who also owns the picturesque Casanova Restaurant in Carmel proper. Tasting is civilized here, even if the old adobe building is rustic.

4 Pilot Road, Carmel Valley | 831/659-1050 | georiswine.com

6 | TALBOTT VINEYARDS

Although the visitor center is in Carmel Valley Village, Talbott owns much vineyard land in the Salinas Valley, including in the Santa Lucia Highlands. The Chardonnays they pour in this homelike stone tasting room (with an often-sunny patio) show that pedigree.

53 West Carmel Valley Road, Carmel Valley | 831/659-3500 | talbottvineyards.com

7 | BERNARDUS WINERY AND VINEYARD

Sister operation to the indulgent lodge, Bernardus Winery is the largest producer of Carmel Valley wines, and its renditions are getting better and better. In the pleasant tasting room in the Village, try the Marinus Bordeaux-style blend—a treat.

5 West Carmel Valley Road, Carmel Valley | 831/659-1900 | bernardus.com

Asilomar State Beach & Conference Center

Spanish Bay

Point Pinos

Cypress Point

17- Mile Dr

Monarch Butterfly Grove

Pacific Grove

Monterey Bay Aquarium

Monterey Bay

Pebble Beach

17- Mile Dr

(68)

Monterey

Carmel Bay

(1)

Fisherman's Wharf

El Estero Park

Carmel

(1)

Seaside

Point Lobos

Mission San Carlos Borromeo del Rio Carmelo

(1)

Carmel River SB

(68)

(218)

Jacks Peak County Park

Point Lobos SR

(1)

Carmel Highlands

Carmel Valley Rd

(68)

CARMEL VALLEY

Carmel River

San Jose Creek

Palo Corona

Garland Ranch Regional Park

Robinson Canyon Rd

Pinyon Peak

Laureles Grade

White Rock Ridge

Carmel Valley Rd

Carmel Valley

N

0   2

Miles

THINGS TO DO

17-MILE DRIVE

A modest entry fee lets you see how the other half lives on this spectacular road, where views of the Pacific vie with views of multimillion-dollar Pebble Beach mansions framed by Monterey cypresses.

Entrances in Carmel and Pacific Grove.

KAYAKING

Monterey Bay Kayaks leads beginner-friendly guided tours into Monterey Bay.

693 Del Monte Avenue, Monterey | 800/649-5357 | montereybaykayaks.com

MISSION SAN CARLOS BORROMEO DEL RÍO CARMELO

Aka Carmel Mission, and just beautiful. Father Junipero Serra is buried here.

3080 Rio Road, Carmel | 831/624-1271 | carmelmission.org

MONTEREY BAY AQUARIUM

Without a doubt, the best aquarium in the nation. 10–6 daily; $22, $13 ages 3–12.

886 Cannery Row, Monterey | 831/648-4888 | montereybayaquarium.org

POINT LOBOS STATE RESERVE

Dramatically windswept point of rock piercing the Pacific. 1.4-mile North Shore Trail offers the best look at the reserve's coves and forests. 9–7 daily; $8 per vehicle.

831/624-4909 | pointlobos.org

TOR HOUSE

Poet Robinson Jeffers built this rugged house (and adjoining Hawk Tower) out of boulders pulled up from the shore at Carmel Bay. Today it's a romantic echo of Carmel's early days as a bohemian retreat.

26304 Ocean View Avenue, Carmel | 831/624-1813 | torhouse.org

WHERE TO EAT

BOUCHÉE RESTAURANT AND WINE BAR

Among Carmel's best splurges, Bouchée offers elevated California cuisine and an ample wine list. Don't forget to check out its wine shop next door.

Mission Street between Ocean and Seventh, Carmel | 831/626-7880 | boucheecarmel.com

CAFE RUSTICA

Enjoy wood-fired pizzas in the lovely outdoor dining area.

10 Delfino Place, Carmel Valley | 831/659-4444

FRESH CREAM

Haute (mostly French) cuisine and gorgeous Monterey Bay views.

99 Pacific Street, Monterey | 831/375-9788 | freshcream.com

JOHN PISTO'S WHALING STATION

Hearty and convivial: big steaks and a bustling atmosphere off Cannery Row.

763 Wave Street, Monterey | 831/373-3778 | whalingstationmonterey.com

KURT'S CARMEL CHOP HOUSE

An unassuming exterior belies the elegance—and the great steaks and downright encyclopedic wine list—within.

Fifth and San Carlos, Carmel | 831/625-1199 | carmelchophouse.com

L'AUBERGE

Intimate (12 tables) and expensive, but worth it for a special occasion. Lucky diners can choose from a 4,500-bottle wine collection.

Monte Verde at Seventh, Carmel | 831/624-8578 | laubergecarmel.com

PASSIONFISH

Locals go here for the fresh seafood that's exclusively from sustainable sources.

701 Lighthouse Avenue, Pacific Grove | 831/655-3311 | passionfish.net

TARPY'S ROADHOUSE

A few minutes east of town, this rambling stone building—once a ranch house—makes for good family dining, with a varied California menu and pretty patios.

2999 Monterey-Salinas Highway, Monterey | 831/647-1444 | tarpys.com

WILL'S FARGO

You'll feel like a Carmel Valley native at this popular "Dining House & Saloon," where the menu rambles from steaks to rack of lamb.

16 West Carmel Valley Road, Carmel Valley | 831/659-2774 | willsfargo.com

PLACES TO STAY

BERNARDUS LODGE AND WINERY

Lots of resorts promise upscale Tuscany in California, but Bernardus and its excellent Marinus restaurant deliver. 57 rooms from $275.

415 Carmel Valley Road, Carmel Valley | 888/648-9463 | bernardus.com

BEST WESTERN CARMEL MISSION INN

Pleasant motel near Carmel Mission and beach. 165 rooms from $99.

3665 Rio Road, Carmel | 800/348-9090 | carmelmissioninn.com

CARMEL VALLEY LODGE

Pleasant, quiet, not too pricey. 31 rooms from $159.

Carmel Valley Road at Ford Road, Carmel Valley | 800/641-4646 | valleylodge.com

CENTRALLA HOTEL

A Victorian-era boardinghouse is now a fine bed-and-breakfast, more or less in the heart of Pacific Grove. 26 rooms from $99.

612 Central Avenue, Pacific Grove | 800/653-5495 | centrellainn.com

CYPRESS INN

Canine heaven: a cozy Spanish Colonial hotel that lets you vacation with your pooch, be it Chihuahua or St. Bernard. 44 rooms from $125.

Lincoln Street and Seventh Avenue, Carmel | 831/624-3871 | cypress-inn.com

LA PLAYA HOTEL

Lush gardens, ocean views, and a century of history make La Playa one of the most elegant places to stay in Carmel. 75 rooms from $180.

Camino Real at Eighth, Carmel | 800/582-8900 | laplayahotel.com

LOS LAURELES LODGE

A former Vanderbilt stable with considerable country charm. 31 rooms from $87.

313 West Carmel Valley Road, Carmel Valley | 800/533-4404 | loslaureles.com

MONTEREY PLAZA HOTEL

Large, well-appointed hotel alongside Monterey Bay. 294 rooms from $200.

400 Cannery Row, Monterey | 831/646-1700 | montereyplazahotel.com

MISSION RANCH

Clint Eastwood's Carmel resort is a charmer, a collection of historic buildings (the farmhouse dates from the 1850s) turned into an easygoing resort with a killer view of Point Lobos. The Sunday jazz brunch is a favorite. 31 rooms from $110.

**26270 Dolores Street, Carmel | 800/538-8221 |
missionranchcarmel.com**

OLD MONTEREY INN

A Tudor-revival home turned into a handsome inn. 10 rooms from $210.

**500 Martin Street, Monterey | 831/375-8284 |
oldmontereyinn.com**

QUAIL LODGE

This nicely updated '60s lodge is a golfers' haven. 97 rooms from $280.

8205 Valley Greens Drive, Carmel | 888/828-8787 | quaillodge.com

TRADEWINDS CARMEL

Streams and bamboo make it a bit of Bali in Carmel. 28 rooms from $325.

**Mission Street at Third, Carmel | 800/624-6665 |
tradewindscarmel.com**

SPOTLIGHT BIG SUR

With its hidden coves, redwood canyons, and views of the steep Santa Lucia Mountains plunging into the blue Pacific, the 90-mile Big Sur coastline is—we're going to be firm about this—the most beautiful in the world. ☆ Twisting California Highway 1 follows the coast for its full length. Along the way are **Andrew Molera** and **Pfeiffer Big Sur** state parks (831/667-2315; reserve america.com), shrines to self-improvement such as Esalen (831/667-3005; esalen.org), and lodging that ranges from soulfully rustic **Deetjen's Big Sur Inn** (831/667-2376; deetjens.com) to plush yet outdoorsy **Treebones Resort** (877/424-4787; treebonesresort.com) to ethereally high-end **Ventana Inn** (831/667-2331; ventana inn.com) to environmentally luxe **Post Ranch Inn** (800/527-2200; postranchinn.com). Oh, and the most beautifully situated restaurant in the world, **Nepenthe** (831/667-2345; nepenthebigsur.com). ☆ For more info, visit bigsurcalifornia.org or call 831/667-2100.

SALINAS VALLEY WINERIES

8 | TASTE OF MONTEREY

The Salinas sibling of the Monterey tasting room is also well worth a visit.

127 Main Street, Salinas | 831/751-1980 | tasteofmonterey.com

9 | MARILYN REMARK WINERY

Joel Burnstein and Marilyn Remark are newer-comers to the Monterey wine scene and have concentrated on Rhône varieties: Roussanne, Marsanne, and Viognier on the white side; Syrah, Grenache, and Petite Sirah on the red.

645 River Road, Salinas | 831/455-9310 | remarkwines.com

10 | PESSAGNO WINERY

Steve Pessagno and his partners bought this Santa Lucia Highlands winery in 2005, opened their tasting room on the River Road corridor, and now produces wines from many of the region's best vineyards—Garys' and Sleepy Hollow among them.

1645 River Road, Salinas | 831/675-9463 | www.pessagnowines.com

11 | BLACKSTONE

Enough wine for the masses is crushed here in Blackstone's Salinas Valley facility (there's a Blackstone in Sonoma County too), but in the large-scale tasting room—past a picturesque duck pond—you'll also find surprisingly good upper-tier wines.

850 South Alta Street, Gonzales | 831/675-5341 | blackstonewinery.com

12 | CHALONE VINEYARD

Winemaking started here high on the slopes of the Gabilan Range in the 1920s, but it was Dick Graff who revived Chalone wineries in the 1970s and '80s. Recently bought by Diageo, it's worth the drive up winding Highway 146 for the the signature Chardonnays.

Highway 146 and Stonewall Canyon Road, Soledad | 831/678-1717 | chalonevineyard.com

13 | HAHN ESTATES/SMITH AND HOOK

The creation of Swiss-born Nicky Hahn, this is a wonderful setting with great views of the Salinas Valley. Focus is on the wines from the Santa Lucia Highlands appellation.

37700 Foothill Road, Soledad | 831/678-4555 | hahnestates.com

14 | PARAISO VINEYARDS

The Smith family has been growing great Santa Lucia Highlands grapes for decades—since before neighboring Garys' and Pisoni Vineyards made the tiny AVA famous. Their own Pinots are now giving the two Garys' Pinots a run for the money.

38060 Paraiso Springs Road, Soledad | 831/678-0300 | paraisovineyards.com

THING TO DO

NATIONAL STEINBECK CENTER

California's only Nobel laureate in literature gets his due. A must-see.

1 Main Street, Salinas | 831/796-3833 | steinbeck.org

WHERE TO EAT

FIRST AWAKENINGS

Breakfast and brunch nirvana thanks to the superior pancakes and omelets.

171 Main Street, Salinas | 831/784-1125

SALINAS VALLEY FISH HOUSE

The Pacific is but a few miles away, and fish here is nicely prepared and very fresh.

172 Main Street, Salinas | 831/775-0175 | salinasvalleyfishhouse.com

PLACE TO STAY

INN AT THE PINNACLES

An inviting retreat high above the Salinas Valley. 6 rooms from $200.

32025 Stonewall Canyon Road, Soledad | 831/678-2400 | innatthepinnacles.com

SPOTLIGHT PAIRING WINE AND ARTICHOKES

Artichokes love Monterey County—the thorny yet succulent vegetable (okay, thistle) thrives in the fog-cooled fields off Monterey Bay. Monterey County also produces superb wines. And herein lies a dilemma: Few foods are harder to pair with wine than artichokes. It's a question of chemistry. The cynarin in the plant makes everything you taste immediately after seem sweeter—not a good effect on wine. ☆ To pull off a good pairing, choose an extremely crisp (high-acid), dry white like Sauvignon Blanc. An herby, lemony mayonnaise or aioli dip picks up on the green flavors in the wine, while the fat tames the cynarin and the wine's acidity cuts through the fat. Or brush cooked artichokes with olive oil and throw them on the grill. The smokiness can be a bridge to juicy reds like Pinot Noir (no shortage of good ones here). Add the 'chokes to a dish with mushrooms and other earth-vegetables, and the deal is sealed.

SAN BENITO WINERIES

15 | LÉAL VINEYARDS

When former fencing contractor Frank Léal tasted his first Chardonnay (2000, Central Coast appellation), after the usual "honeyed, tropical, creamy" comments, he declared, "This wine is the shiznit!" The phrase is still on the labels of this up-and-coming winery.

300 Maranatha Drive, Hollister | 831/636-1023 | lealvineyards.com

16 | DEROSE VINEYARDS

Some of the big, rustic wines here come from vines planted before 1900. One of the most exotic is Negrette, an old French variety (rare even in France now) once called Pinot St. George. DeRose partners bought some of the old Almaden's vineyard land, along with that winery's huge underground wine cellar.

9970 Cienega Road, Hollister | 831/636-9143 (call for appointment) | derosewine.com

17 | PIETRA SANTA WINERY

The grandest of all the wineries in the county, Tuscan-style Pietra Santa—also on an old Almaden Winery parcel—was the creation of second-generation Italian-American Joseph Gimelli, who added Dolcetto, Sangiovese, and Pinot Grigio to the region's grape lineup. Word has it that the new owners are planting Pinot. The view from the second-story tasting room is pretty spectacular.

10034 Cienega Road, Hollister | 831/636-1991 | pietrasantawinery.com

18 | CALERA WINE COMPANY

Somewhat remote, Calera's vineyards are the only ones in San Benito's limestone-rich Mt. Harlan AVA—just 20 miles or so across the Gabilan range from Chalone. Owner Josh Jensen manages to make a range of single-vineyard Pinot Noirs that are consistently rated among the best in the state—in a place most wine drinkers have never heard of. In his gravity-flow winery, which you can visit, he handles the wines as little as possible: His Pinots have a Burgundian soul.

11300 Cienega Road, Hollister | 831/637-9170 | calerawine.com

19 | FLINT WINE CELLARS

Scott Flint, former assistant winemaker for Josh Jensen at Calera Wine Company, has struck out on his own to produce great Pinot Noir with the same Calera values—natural nuances from as little handling of the wine as possible. Visiting and tasting here is a homey, personal encounter.

13160 Cienega Road, Hollister | 831/636-8986 (call for appointment)

THING TO DO

OLD MISSION SAN JUAN BAUTISTA

In continuous use from 1812, this is the mission made famous in *Vertigo*.

Second and Mariposa Streets, San Juan Bautista | 831/623-4528 | oldmissionsjb.org

WHERE TO EAT

INN AT TRES PINOS

South of San Juan Bautista, a handsome roadhouse serving fine Italian food.

6991 Airline Highway, Tres Pinos | 831/628-3320

JARDINES DE SAN JUAN

Go here for the lovely gardens, powerful margaritas, and good Mexican food.

115 Third Street, San Juan Bautista | 831/623-4466 | jardinesrestaurant.com

PLACE TO STAY

POSADA DE SAN JUAN

A Mission-style motel in the historic heart of town. 34 rooms from $98.

310 Fourth Street, San Juan Bautista | 831/623-4030

SPOTLIGHT PINNACLES NATIONAL MONUMENT

If you're touring the wineries of the Salinas Valley or San Benito County, Pinnacles National Monument (5000 Highway 146, Paicines; 831/389-4485; nps.gov/pinn) makes a great detour. Straddling the crest of the Gabilan Range, it's the most impressive collection of rocks in California. ☆ The pinnacles of Pinnacles are eroded remnants of an ancient volcano, dragged here from Southern California by the San Andreas Fault. The park contains 30 miles of hiking trails—look up and you may see a California condor. ☆ You can reach Pinnacles from its west side at Soledad via Highway 146, or enter from the east by taking Highway 25 south from Hollister to Highway 146. Spring is particularly fine, when the drama of the rocks is equaled by the displays of lupine, poppies, and other wildflowers.

SAN LUIS OBISPO

WHEN WILLIAM RANDOLPH HEARST—arguably San Luis Obispo County's most famous resident—built his rococo castle on the San Luis coast, he included a substantial wine cellar, protected by iron doors, that he filled with French and German vintages. It's a good thing Hearst wasn't building San Simeon today. San Luis Obispo County has become such a stellar wine region, he'd need all of his castle's 165 rooms to hold the superb Syrahs and Viogniers being produced right around him.

The county contains three main appellations and a small one, York Mountain. Due east across the Santa Lucia Mountains from San Simeon spreads the largest, the 610,000-acre Paso Robles AVA. Few wine areas in California have changed as much or as rapidly as this sprawling land of rolling, oak-dotted hills. Twenty years ago, it was cattle country, with fewer than 10 wineries. Today it's home to nearly 200.

And no other California wine region is as hard to characterize as Paso Robles. There's just too much of it. The unifying condition is that it's warm here, but not as hot in its warmest parts as many people think, and cool enough in other parts to surprise outsiders.

Two features determine temperature and wine-growing potential. The Santa Lucia Range blocks the cool ocean air from the stretch of the region east of the Salinas River (and Highway 101). In broad strokes, the east side, as it's known, is the hot, dry land of Cabs from large producers like Meridian; some, like J. Lohr, do it especially well. On average, the east side temperature drops 40 degrees at night during the growing season, giving the area one of the greatest diurnal swings in California (propitious for wine). There's a crack in the range, though, called the

Continues page 118 >

SUGGESTED ROUTES

☆ **PASO ROBLES** *The region is an ideal weekend destination: Tour wineries to the east of town one day, wineries in the mountains west of town on the other. The Paso Robles Inn makes a good base, but the luxurious Carlton Hotel in Atascadero is another possibility, and it's convenient to the more southerly wineries.*

☆ **EDNA VALLEY AND ARROYO GRANDE VALLEY** *These linked regions are an easy half-day or day trip out of San Luis Obispo or the Pismo Beach area.*

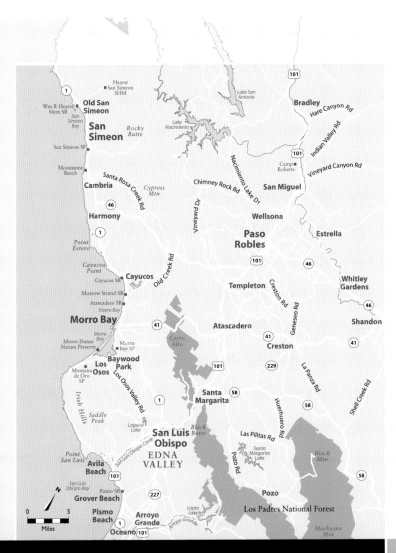

Templeton Gap, which lets those maritime breezes funnel into the west side of the Paso Robles AVA. Here, small producers are crafting Syrahs and white Rhône varieties that are among the best in the state.

As you might expect, an east side/west side rivalry—at times it feels almost like a class system—is detectable, though much denied, in Paso Robles. In any event, geographically based judgments are way too simple. Many west-side winemakers get some of their grapes from growers on the east side, and vice versa. And all the reds here—Zinfandels, Cabs, Syrahs—share rich color, soft tannins, and ripe, juicy fruit flavors.

As the region's hillsides went from nurturing cattle to nurturing Syrah and Cabernet, the towns changed too. For decades the classic California ranch town, Paso Robles—call it "Paso" if you want to sound like a local—now holds stylish wine bars and French restaurants that coexist with the feed stores and saddleries. Two wineries have posh inns that let you sleep, luxuriously, among the vines. Tiny Templeton has a first-class restaurant, Atascadero an excellent hotel.

The county's other main appellations—Edna Valley and Arroyo Grande Valley—are more compact, stretching south from the city of San

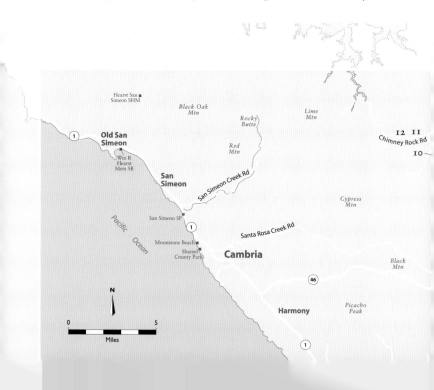

Luis Obispo. Here the maritime influence is more noticeable, steering winemakers toward Chardonnays and Pinot Noirs—their versions are joining the leagues of the best in California. As in Paso Robles, these are easy wineries to tour. Wine is taken seriously but not solemnly, and odds are good you'll find the winemaker in the tasting room when you visit.

PASO ROBLES WINERIES

I | MARTIN & WEYRICH

A Tuscan showplace to match the owners' Villa Toscana inn (or maybe it's the other way around), Martin & Weyrich has a corner on Italian varieties in the area, and a couple of firsts to its credit: It was the first to produce a Nebbiolo and a "super-Tuscan"–style blend of Cab and Sangiovese.

2610 Buena Vista Drive, Paso Robles | 805/238-2520 | **martinweyrich.com**

2 | GARRETSON WINE COMPANY

If Gary Eberle is Mr. Syrah, Mat Garretson is Mr. Viognier. In fact, Garretson came to this region to be Eberle's sales and marketing director, and the Viognier Guild he had founded

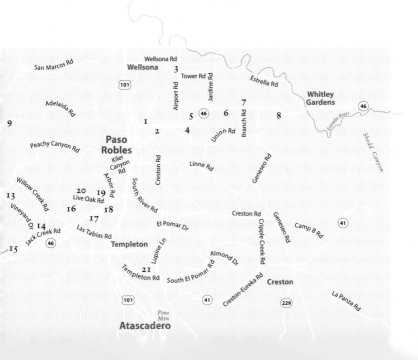

earlier grew into Paso's Hospice du Rhône, the biggest international festival of Rhône wines in the world (in early May each year). Garretson's red and white Rhône wines are getting a lot of well-deserved attention in his modest facility on the east side.

2323 Tuley Court, Suite 110, Paso Robles ⏐ 805/239-2074 ⏐ mrviognier.com

3 ⏐ J. LOHR VINEYARDS & WINERY

The number of barrels stacked in the cavernous barrel rooms at J. Lohr is mind-boggling —this is a behemoth producer. But Jerry Lohr, who first grew a lot of wine in Monterey County before digging in deeply here, is a major promoter of Paso Robles as a region and a community, and his wines generally deliver an awful lot for the money. Make a point to taste some from the family's Hilltop Vineyard.

6169 Airport Road, Paso Robles ⏐ 805/239-8900 ⏐ jlohr.com

4 ⏐ ROBERT HALL WINERY

Another arched showplace on the east side, Robert Hall has state-of-the-art space and equipment, 19,000 square feet of caves, and plenty of characteristic chocolate notes in its Merlot. The wraparound tasting bar gives way outside to a panoramic terrace and two bocce courts.

3443 Mill Road, Paso Robles ⏐ 805/239-1616 ⏐ roberthallwinery.com

5 ⏐ EBERLE WINERY

Visionary, general character, and now a Paso Robles institution, Gary Eberle is a major reason Syrah is growing in California—he practically introduced the grape into the state. His winery on the east side now has 16,000 square feet of caves underneath, which you can tour, and a great sweeping view from the deck, which you can picnic on.

3.5 miles east of Highway 101 on Highway 46 East, Paso Robles ⏐ 805/238-9607 ⏐ eberlewinery.com

6 ⏐ EOS ESTATE WINERY

With the look of a Mediterranean monastery and a name inspired by the Greek goddess of dawn, EOS is one of Paso's more ambitiously elegant east-side facilities (sister label Aciero Family Vineyards is also here). The 6,000-square-foot visitor center bills itself as a marketplace, with a wide range of goods and treats; a large rose garden and picnic area make it tempting to stick around and enjoy some of them. Try the EOS "Tears of Dew" late-harvest Moscato.

5625 Highway 46 East, Paso Robles ⏐ 805/239-2562 ⏐ eosvintage.com

7 ⏐ MERIDIAN VINEYARDS

There's hardly a soul alive in this country who doesn't know of Meridian—mostly from its multithousands of cases per year of "Central Coast" Chardonnay and the like. Paso's east side is the source of much of that juice. In the picturesque stone winery, you can taste some limited-release wines not available in grocery stores, and picnic on the beautiful grounds.

7000 Highway 46 East, Paso Robles | 805/226-7133 | meridianvineyards.com

8 | TOBIN JAMES CELLARS

In Paso Robles start-up style, Tobin James began making his own wines while working in other cellars. Now he makes many, and they have an enthusiastic following. Taste them at his antique bar about 8 miles east of town, out Highway 46, where the stage-coach used to stop (the building has been restored).

8950 Union Road, Paso Robles | 805/239-2204 | tobinjames.com

9 | ADELAIDA CELLARS

Named for a farming community dating to the late 1800s, Adelaida is one of the few Paso wineries becoming known for Pinot Noir (from the HMR Vineyard). Shows just how cool it can get in these wildish hills west of Highway 101. The winery, with its name scripted on the outside of the building and its pleasant tiled tasting room inside, sits at 1,800 feet in the Santa Lucia Mountains.

5805 Adelaida Road, Paso Robles | 805/239-8980 | adelaida.com

10 | TABLAS CREEK VINEYARD

Many Paso vintners are working with Rhône grapes, but only Tablas Creek is co-owned by a real Rhône wine family—the Perrins, who own the famous Château Beaucastel in Châteauneuf-du-Pâpe. Along with the wine-importing Haas family, they saw great potential in Paso Robles for their varieties, and the white and red blends are very, very good. Visit the tasting room anytime or call ahead to tour the winery's vine nursery, which specializes in Rhône varietals.

9339 Adelaida Road, Paso Robles | 805/237-1231 | tablascreek.com

11 | CARMODY MCNIGHT ESTATE WINES

Actor and artist Gary Conway (whose birth name is Carmody) and former Miss America Marian Conway (whose maiden name is McKnight) made their first wine in the cellar of this 130-year-old lakeside farmhouse. Browse Conway's color-saturated art inside, then go outside to enjoy some nibbles by the lake.

11240 Chimney Rock Road, Paso Robles | 805/238-9392 | carmodymcknight.com

12 | JUSTIN VINEYARDS & WINERY

Justin and Deborah Baldwin create legendary concentrated wines from their rolling vineyards on the area's far-west side—"Isosceles," a Bordeaux-style blend, routinely sells out. Justin was the first Paso-area winery to break into the *Wine Spectator's* top-100 list. Right in the middle of those vineyards, the Baldwins' small Just Inn is one of the most luxuriously romantic places to stay in the area, and Deborah's Room—the inn's restaurant—yields some of the area's best cooking.

11680 Chimney Rock Road, Paso Robles │
805/238-6932 (call for appointment) │ **justinwine.com**

I3 │ OPOLO VINEYARDS

East meets west at Opolo, whose vineyards can be found on both sides of the highway. Taste cheek by jowl with barrels in the cellar—try the estate "Rhapsody," which has a lot of Cabernet Franc in it.

7110 Vineyard Drive, Paso Robles │ **805/238-9593** │ **opolo.com**

I4 │ DOVER CANYON WINERY

Rebel Rose, a springer spaniel, is in charge of hospitality and parking here, while the image of the late Blue, a white Saint Bernard, graces the labels, a space he earned by once pulling surfing-enthusiast/winery owner Dan Panico to safety after his surfboard had knocked him unconscious. A former winemaker at Eberle, Panico makes very good Rhône varieties and Zinfandels.

4520 Vineyard Drive, Paso Robles │ **805/237-0101** │ **dovercanyon.com**

I5 │ YORK MOUNTAIN WINERY

York Mountain is the oldest continuously operating winery on the Central Coast, and claims its own little AVA (York Mountain). Recently bought by Martin & Weyrich, York Mountain might have changes in the offing, but it's a little pocket of history now, under the oaks on the west side.

7505 York Mountain Road, Templeton │ **805/238-3925** │
yorkmountainwinery.com

I6 │ MIDNIGHT CELLARS

Family-run Midnight Cellars has moved from a horse barn to a new 10,000-square-foot facility, but a visit here still gives you a chance to get close to a small wine operation. Watch the Zinfandel-Syrah blends.

2925 Anderson Road, Paso Robles │ **805/239-8904** │ **midnightcellars.com**

I7 │ CASTORO CELLARS

There are cork trees in the gardens around Castoro's Mediterranean-style tasting room, but they won't be producing real cork anytime soon. The wines inside, however, are self-described as "dam fine."

1315 North Bethel Road, Templeton │ **805/238-0725** │ **castorocellars.com**

1 8 | PEACHY CANYON WINERY

Zinfandel is the signature wine here; don't miss the one labeled "Especial." The Beckett family and their vineyards in Peachy Canyon west of Highway 101 have been in the Paso wine picture since the early 1980s. But the building that houses the tasting room—the Old Bethel School House—goes back to the 1880s.

1480 North Bethel Road, Templeton | **805/239-1918** | **peachycanyon.com**

1 9 | WINDWARD VINEYARD

Windward Vineyard is proof that those Templeton Gap breezes are very cool: Husband-and-wife owners Marc Goldberg and Maggie D'ambrosia make only Pinot Noir here—an anomaly in Paso Robles. They don't produce all that much, but what they do suggests that at least some parts of Paso are brilliant Pinot territory.

1380 Live Oak Road, Paso Robles | **805/239-2565** | **windwardvineyard.com**

2 0 | L'AVENTURE

The adventurer here is Frenchman Stephan Asseo, whose Cabernet and Syrah blends (an almost heretical combination in France, where Bordeaux grapes stay in Bordeaux and Rhône in the Rhône) have become cult wines locally. The tasting room may be small but the critics' scores are high.

2815 Live Oak Road, Paso Robles | **805/227-1588** | **aventurewine.com**

2 1 | WILD HORSE WINERY & VINEYARDS

Located in the Templeton AVA, Wild Horse makes a wide range of wines, including Pinot Noir. It's one of the larger producers in the region now, at close to 150,000 cases a year. But as an early proponent of sustainable winegrowing, and with its range of varietals, Wild Horse still captures the ethos of the Central Coast. Just don't feed the llama; it spits.

1437 Wild Horse Winery Court, Templeton | **805/434-2541** | **wildhorsewinery.com**

FAVORITES & DISCOVERIES ☆ PASO ROBLES

EBERLE WINERY *Owner and winemaker Gary Eberle is the main reason why there's so much great Syrah in California*

TOBIN JAMES CELLARS *This former stagecoach stop is now a must-visit for anyone doing a wine tour of Paso's east side*

JUSTIN VINEYARDS & WINERY *With its terrific concentrated wines, romantic inn, and tasty restaurant, this place has it all*

PEACHY CANYON WINERY *Its been a west-side mainstay since the 1980s, which is a long time for this relatively young region*

THINGS TO DO

CAMBRIA

A straight shot west on Highway 46 from Paso Robles, Cambria does the small-town-on-the-coast thing very well. Its Main Street offers appealing restaurants and galleries, and its coastline—especially Moonstone Beach—is nothing if not picturesque. The town also makes a convenient base for visiting Hearst's Castle. For more information, visit the Chamber of Commerce's offices.

767 Main Street, Cambia | 805/927-3624 | cambriachamber.org

HEARST SAN SIMEON STATE HISTORIC MONUMENT

Paso Robles is so close to Hearst Castle—about 35 miles over Highway 46—that you owe yourself a visit. The wine cellar can be seen on tour four. Reserve tours in advance, especially in summer.

750 Hearst Castle Road, San Simeon | 800/444-4445 | hearstcastle.com

FESTIVALS

The Paso Robles Zinfandel Festival in March includes two auctions. The Wine Festival in May is held in the town's downtown park. Wineries throughout the area host special events of their own during festival weekends.

800/549-9463 | pasowine.com

WHERE TO EAT

BISTRO LAURENT

Hearty French fare in a brick building downtown. Naturally it has a terrific wine list to accompany entrées ranging from scallops to lamb to venison.

1202 Pine Street, Paso Robles | 805/226-8191

MCPHEE'S GRILL

In the onetime railroad town of Templeton, this first-rate restaurant is focused on local ingredients. The oak-grilled steaks are legendary, and the house wines are the handiwork of none other than Santa Barbara winemaker Jim Clendenen.

416 South Main Street, Templeton | 805/434-3204 | mcphees.com

PARIS RESTAURANT

It's a charming curiosity of Paso Robles that the town boasts not one but two good outposts of cuisine Française (Bistro Laurent being the other).

1221 Park Street, Paso Robles | 805/227-4082

PANOLIVO

This popular French-Mediterranean bistro includes a bakery that makes a star-shaped cookie dedicated to winemaker Tobin James.

1344 Park Street, Paso Robles | 805/239-3366 | panolivo.com

VILLA CREEK

On the downtown square, a winemaker's hangout with organic California cuisine.

1144 Pine Street, Paso Robles | 805/238-3000 | villacreek.com

VINOTECA WINE BAR

Cozy spot with a great selection of local wines and weekly special tastings.

835 12th Street, Paso Robles | 805/227-7154 | vinotecawinebar.com

PLACES TO STAY

THE CARLTON HOTEL

Beautifully restored historic hotel in downtown Atascadero. Restaurants include the Carlton Grill, a sushi bar, and a bakery/cafe. 50 rooms from $135.

6005 El Camino Real, Atascadero | 877/204-9830 | the-carlton.com

JUST INN

Sumptuous inn surrounded by the vineyards of Justin Winery. Its excellent restaurant is called Deborah's Room. 4 suites from $325, breakfast included.

11680 Chimney Rock Road, Paso Robles | 800/726-0049 | justinwine.com

PASO ROBLES INN

Handsome, tile-roofed old California–style lodge in downtown Paso Robles. Good steakhouse and coffee shop on premises. 98 rooms from $95.

1103 Spring Street, Paso Robles | 800/676-1713 | pasoroblesinn.com

SUMMERWOOD INN

At Summerwood Winery, a beautiful farmhouse-style inn. 9 rooms from $215.

2175 Arbor Road, Paso Robles | 805/227-1111 | summerwoodwine.com

VILLA TOSCANA

Gorgeous Italian-style inn set among the vineyards of Martin & Weyrich winery. 8 suites from $375.

4230 Buena Vista, Paso Robles | 805/238-5600 | myvillatoscana.com

EDNA VALLEY AND
ARROYO GRANDE WINERIES

1 | BAILEYANA WINERY

Baileyana's tasting room, in the historic Independence Schoolhouse on Orcutt Road, is in direct contrast to its dramatic new winery in Firepeak Vineyard, where Burgundy-born winemaker Christian Roguenant has the best possible conditions and equipment to work with the Chardonnay, Pinot Noir, and Syrah grapes coming off the cool-weather vines at the base of Islay Mountain. The estate also includes the larger, older Paragon Vineyard, but Firepeak is the one to watch. Relax at the schoolhouse's picnic area, where a game of croquet or bocce has been known to break out.

**5828 Orcutt Road, San Luis Obispo | 805/269-8200 |
baileyana.com**

2 | SAUCELITO CANYON

Overshadowed by bigger neighbor Rancho Arroyo Grande, Saucelito Canyon makes Zinfandel that shouldn't be passed by (only about 2,500 cases are produced in any given year). Some of it comes from vines with roots that go back to 1880. In the small tasting room, you can also try wines from a small new Edna Valley producer, Ortman Family Vineyards. Chuck Ortman is a Napa Valley winemaking refugee by way of Meridian Vineyards; he's teamed up with son Matt for a family label.

**3080 Biddle Ranch Road, San Luis Obispo | 805/543-2111, ext. 19 |
saucelitocanyon.com**

3 | EDNA VALLEY VINEYARD

One of the larger producers in the region, Edna Valley Vineyard is probably familiar to Chardonnay lovers. The Chardonnay from the estate's Paragon Vineyard is always good and widely available; the Paragon Syrah is a sleeper—give it a try. All are good values. The Jack Niven Hospitality Center here is one of the favorite stops in the valley, with grand views over Paragon Vineyard to landmark Islay Peak, and winery tours every hour.

**2585 Biddle Ranch Road, San Luis Obispo | 805/544-5855 |
ednavalley.com**

4 | TOLOSA WINERY

Tasting at Tolosa has an air of modern glitz, with wine-related materials built in: cork floor, glass bar, etc. Large windows give you a view into the tank room. Because Tolosa sells or custom-crushes the bulk of grapes from its huge Edna Ranch Vineyard, it has the pick of the crop to choose from for its own limited bottlings, with delicious results (try the Edna Ranch Syrah).

**4910 Edna Road, San Luis Obispo | 805/782-0500 |
tolosawinery.com**

5 | CLAIBORNE & CHURCHILL

The Claiborne & Churchill family-owned winery is unique in its stucco over straw-bale construction, and in its focus on Alsatian whites. It produces plenty of dry Riesling and spicy Gewürztraminer, with a smattering of Chardonnay and other bottlings such as Pinot Noir from grapes grown in the Edna Valley AVA thrown in for good measure. The crisp Riesling is a reminder of what a good wine this noble grape can make (something we're just learning in this country).

2649 Carpenter Canyon Road, San Luis Obispo | **805/544-4066** |
claibornechurchill.com

6 | DOMAINE ALFRED

Owner Terry Speizer knows his vines' taste in music ("the Pinot Noirs like Gregorian chants, but they hate salsa"), and with the range of wines Domaine Alfred produces, he has a lot to keep up with! There's an interesting comparison to be tasted here between an oak-rich California-style Chardonnay and a crisp, minerally Burgundian one. Just about all of the winery's grapes are grown in its Chamisal Vineyard, which was first planted in 1972.

7525 Orcutt Road, San Luis Obispo | **805/541-9463** | **domainealfred.com**

7 | TALLEY VINEYARDS

Drive through the cilantro and bell pepper fields of a third-generation farm to get to Talley's beautiful Chardonnays and Pinot Noirs. Tasting used to happen in the historic El Rincón Adobe on the property, but there's a new room now. The Talley family owns a handful of vineyards in San Luis Obispo County; for our money, Rincon and Rosemary's produce their most compelling wines.

3031 Lopez Drive, Arroyo Grande | 805/489-0446 | talleyvineyards.com

8 | RANCHO ARROYO GRANDE WINERY AND VINEYARDS

This newcomer has made good on the "grande" part of the region's name, with more than 200 acres of vineyards on the beautiful 4,000-acre Rancho Arroyo Grande that was part of the original Spanish land grant. The Rhône blends and Zinfandels show promise. At this writing, the tasting room is open on the first Saturday of every month; other days require an appointment.

591 Hi Mountain Road, Arroyo Grande | 805/489-2855 | ranchoarroyograndewines.com

9 | LAETITIA VINEYARD AND WINERY

One of the larger producers in the region, with an interesting history: Founded in the early 1980s by the French house Champagne Deutz, the winery produced sparkling wine for many years. It still makes a little, but the current owner has turned to still Pinot Noir—a lot of it—solid, good-value wines. Laetitia's upper tiers are often praised by critics, and two of its new stepchildren—the Barnwood and Avila labels—come in with great value again for the mainstream (where we all swim most of the time). Many options, in this view-rich hilltop visitor center off Highway 101.

453 Laetitia Vineyard Drive, Arroyo Grande | 805/481-1772 | laetitiawine.com

THINGS TO DO

ARROYO GRANDE

Branch Street, center of old Arroyo Grande, is a pleasantly walkable collection of cafes and shops. Get maps at the Visitor and Tourism Center.

117 $^1/_2$ Branch Street | 805/473-2250 | arroyograndevillage.org

SAN LUIS OBISPO

Centered along Higuera Creek, San Luis Obispo's downtown is one of the most appealing in California. Must-sees include Mission San Luis Obispo de Tolosa on Palm Street and a terrific Thursday night farmers' market along Higuera Street.

WHERE TO EAT

CAFÉ ROMA

Rustic and Italian, with a good selection of local wines.

**1020 Railroad Avenue, San Luis Obispo | 805/541-6800 |
caferomaslo.com**

FIALA'S GOURMET CAFÉ

The only eatery in Edna Valley has good omelets, paninis, and picnic fixings.

1653 Old Price Canyon Road, San Luis Obispo | 805/543-1313

KOBERL AT BLUE

"Terroir cuisine" featuring Central Coast ingredients and wines, plus evening jazz.

998 Monterey Street, San Luis Obispo | 805/783-1185

NOVO RESTAURANT

Go here for food with Brazilian and Mediterranean influences.

**726 Higuera Street, San Luis Obispo | 805/543-3986 |
novorestaurant.com**

TASTE

This wine bar lets you sample vintages from Edna and Arroyo Grande valleys.

1003 Osos Street, San Luis Obispo | 805/269-8278 | taste-slo.com

PLACES TO STAY

GARDEN STREET INN BED AND BREAKFAST

In downtown San Luis Obispo, an 1887 Queen Anne home turned into a lovely little inn. 9 rooms and 4 suites from $155.

**1212 Garden Street, San Luis Obispo | 805/545-9802 |
gardenstreetinn.com**

PETIT SOLEIL BED AND BREAKFAST

Provence-style inn in downtown SLO. 15 rooms from $139.

**1473 Monterey Street, San Luis Obispo | 805/549-0321 |
petitsoleilslo.com**

SAN LUIS CREEK LODGE

Traditionally styled hotel about 1 mile from downtown. 25 rooms from $149.

**1941 Monterey Street, San Luis Obispo | 805/541-1122 |
sanluiscreeklodge.com**

SANTA BARBARA

EVERY ROAD INTO SANTA BARBARA'S wine country is beautiful, but maybe the most beautiful of all is Highway 154, which climbs north over the San Marcos Pass from the city of Santa Barbara. The highway crests, and there, below you, past the blue squiggle of Lake Cachuma, spreads the valley: green, walled on three sides by castellated mountains, and stretching mistily west to the Pacific.

Given its scenery, its proximity to Santa Barbara and Los Angeles, and the fact that it now produces some world-class wines, you might think the Santa Ynez Valley and its adjacent (and even more promising) appellations, Santa Rita Hills and Santa Maria Valley, had been wine centers for aeons. In fact, for much of its history, Santa Barbara's wine country was the Southern California version of the Old West: a loping land of cattle ranches and horse farms, where Los Rancheros Visitadores— a well-heeled posse of CEOs and politicians—galloped through on horseback, re-enacting the era of the caballero.

Not until the 1970s did pioneering winemakers like Richard Sanford see the potential for growing wine here and start planting vineyards. They saw a series of interconnected valleys that—unusual in California—run east to west, with rugged mountain ranges on three sides but open to the Pacific Ocean to the west. The offshore current here is much colder than it is in the city of Santa Barbara itself, just to the south; dramatically cooling fog blows inland. Roughly speaking, for every mile you travel east from the coast, the average temperature rises by one degree.

Three main valleys are the wine beneficiaries of this marine influence: Santa Ynez, Santa Maria, and the Santa Rita Hills (*Sunset* magazine's Up-and-Coming Wine Region of the Year in 2006). The easternmost, and therefore warmest, Santa Ynez Valley is the most varied in terms of tasting rooms and grapes. Early celebrity owners, like Fess Parker and the Firestone family, made this the tourist destination of choice, with large, merchandise-rich tasting rooms and arrays of value-priced wines. Zaca Mesa, also a longtime player here, has launched many good Syrahs into the world (as well as a fair number of winemakers). Newer-comers—Beckman, Stolpman—are now making their marks in the wine world. The grapes that seem to do best in the Santa Ynez Valley are Bordeaux

Continues page 132 >

SUGGESTED ROUTES

☆ **FOXEN CANYON** *Explore the wineries of Santa Maria Valley, then follow Foxen Canyon Road south to Santa Ynez*

☆ **SANTA RITA HILLS** *Begin in Buellton, head east on Highway 246 to Lompoc, then return via scenic Santa Rosa Road*

☆ **SANTA YNEZ TRIANGLE** *Highway 246 between Solvang and Santa Ynez; Highway 154 between Santa Ynez and Los Olivos; Alamo Pintado Road between Los Olivos and Solvang*

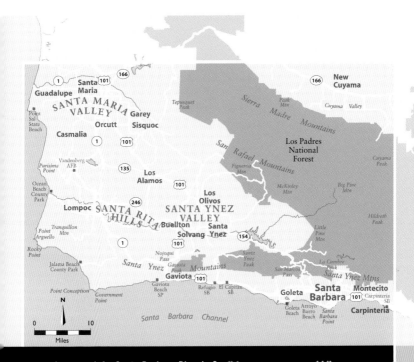

varieties—Cabernet Sauvignon, Merlot, and Sauvignon Blanc—with some Rhônes to watch as well, notably Syrah and Grenache.

In contrast, the Santa Maria Valley, to the west, is much colder and its output more focused. Chardonnay and Pinot Noir are the main grapes here. Larger-than-life winemaker Jim Clendenen of Au Bon Climat has put them on the map. But because the vineyards in this valley tend to be enormous and some of the most interesting producers not open to the public (Au Bon Climat and Qupé among them), wine touring here is a little more challenging.

The biggest news recently has been in the Santa Rita Hills, south of Santa Maria. This newest AVA is as cold as its neighbor to the north but has different soils. Richard Sanford saw its potential when he planted his original vineyard here, and now a fresh collection of talent is putting in (and producing exciting versions of) Pinot Noir, Chardonnay, and Syrah: Melville, Fiddlehead, Sea Smoke, and, the holy grail, Brewer-Clifton (Greg Brewer is also Melville's winemaker). Tasting in the Santa Rita Hills has become exciting, and a cluster of vintners in Lompoc have made the town a hot address for Pinot Noir.

Today, thanks in part to the film *Sideways*—which got the whole region's mix of sophistication and unpretentiousness right—and the raft of Hollywood celebrities who have landed in the vicinity, Santa Barbara wine country is no longer undiscovered. That fact is readily apparent in the growing number of first-rate inns and restaurants, not to mention the property values. Still, the region holds on to a lot of its earlier, slower-paced charms. The little town of Solvang remains as determinedly Danish as ever, even if wine-tasting rooms threaten to outnumber bakeries down-town. Los Olivos's Grand Avenue has become an outpost of chic restaurants and galleries—but they still share the avenue with Jedlicka's tack and saddle shop.

In theory, it's possible to tour Santa Barbara County's wine country as a day trip out of Santa Barbara. But that would be rushing things. Better to take a couple of days to enjoy the drive along Foxen Canyon Road (one of the most beautifully rewarding wine routes in California) and the rustic charms of the town of Santa Ynez—in short, to experience a region that on a green spring afternoon can seem like paradise on earth.

SANTA YNEZ WINERIES

1 | SANTA BARBARA WINERY

The oldest winery in the county (it was only established in 1962) is also a cozy place to taste solid Pinot Noirs and Chardonnays against a backdrop of barrels, without leaving the city of Santa Barbara. Many of the winery's grapes are from the respected Lafond Vineyard in the Santa Rita Hills.

202 Anacapa Street, Santa Barbara | 805/963-3633 | sbwinery.com

2 | GAINEY VINEYARD

If your taste runs to rich wines, this lovely tiled Spanish-style tasting room is the place for you. Gainey has come to be known for its Chardonnay, produced in the generously oaked California style. Enjoy a bottle at one of the picnic tables in the vineyard garden.

3950 East Highway 246, Santa Ynez | 805/688-0558 | gaineyvineyard.com

3 | SANTA YNEZ INN WINE CELLAR

This tasting room next door to the Santa Ynez Inn specializes in wineries like Au Bon Climat, which are highly regarded but have no tasting facilities of their own.

3631 Sagunto Street, Santa Ynez | 805/688-8688 | santaynezwinecellar.com

4 | THE BRANDER VINEYARD

Enjoy getting an education in the many faces of Sauvignon Blanc produced at this pink mini-château, with its wood-beamed ceilings and tiled floors. Our favorite: Au Naturel, made without any oak, for pure Sauvignon Blanc flavor.

2401 Refugio Road, Los Olivos | 805/688-2455 | brander.com

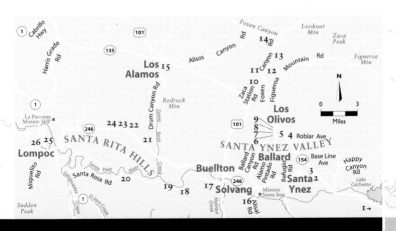

5 | BECKMEN VINEYARDS

Try Beckmen's Grenache, Syrah, and other Rhône varieties from the promising Purisima Mountain Vineyard. Picnic in a gazebo near the duck pond.

2670 Ontiveros Road, Los Olivos | 805/688-8664 | beckmenvineyards.com

6 | LOS OLIVOS CAFE & WINE MERCHANT

Two quests can be satisfied at once in this bustling establishment: one for a good lunch or dinner, the other for an interesting wine, including varieties from Qupé.

2879 Grand Avenue, Los Olivos | 805/688-7265 | losolivoscafe.com

7 | ANDREW MURRAY VINEYARDS

Andrew Murray's is another tasting room that makes Los Olivos one of the best sipping towns in the county. Syrah is the thing here, and at decent prices compared to the trend for highly rated bottles.

2901-A Grand Avenue, Los Olivos | 805/686-9604 | andrewmurrayvineyards.com

8 | THE LOS OLIVOS TASTING ROOM & WINE SHOP

Located just outside of town, this intimate, rustic tasting room and shop in Los Olivos's original 1887 general store is a home for local wines from makers who don't have tasting rooms of their own.

2905 Grand Avenue, Los Olivos | 805/688-7406 | losolivoswines.com

9 | RICHARD LONGORIA WINES

History and winemaking come together in Longoria's metal-sided tasting room, in what was a machine shop in the early 1900s. Richard Longoria made wine for others in the valley (like Firestone and Gainey) for more than 20 years before going full-time with his own label. Enjoy the patio and garden, as well as the fountains (they're for sale).

2935 Grand Avenue, Los Olivos | 866/759-4637 | longoriawine.com

10 | FIRESTONE VINEYARD

The warm, mural-crowned room that houses the Firestone family's wines is an inviting place to taste—try the dry Riesling. The picnic possibilities outside are even more exciting.

5000 Zaca Station Road, Los Olivos | 805/688-3940 | firestonewine.com

11 | CURTIS WINERY

Curtis is the up-and-coming offshoot of Firestone, specializing in Syrah and fellow Rhône grapes. Set in the middle of beautiful oaks, the winery has a tasting room that gets you right into the cellar. And the fee here includes a tasting at Firestone as well.

Zaca Station Road, Los Olivos (1/4 mile east of Firestone) | 805/686-8999 | curtiswinery.com

12 | KOEHLER WINERY

This newcomer to the Foxen Canyon Wine Trail lineup can claim some of the prettiest grounds. The vines have been here for several decades, being pressed into good wine under other labels. Now, Kory Koehler aims to harness the quality for her own label.

5360 Foxen Canyon Road, Los Olivos | 805/693-8384 | koehlerwinery.com

13 | FESS PARKER WINERY & VINEYARDS

The large gift shop at this celebrity-owned winery might be big on coonskin caps and wine toppers, but the wines poured at the sleek tasting bar are getting beyond commercial quality these days.

6200 Foxen Canyon Road, Los Olivos | 800/841-1104 | fessparker.com

14 | ZACA MESA WINERY & VINEYARD

Beautiful grounds, propitious picnic spots and paths, and Rhône wines—our favorites are the dry rosé, called Z Gris, and the rich Black Bear Block Syrah. More than a few vintners in the area got their start at Zaca Mesa, including Jim Clendenen of Au Bon Climat.

6905 Foxen Canyon Road, Los Olivos | 805/688-9339, ext. 308 | zacamesa.com

15 | BEDFORD THOMPSON WINERY & VINEYARD

Cabernet Franc is one of the most distinctive wines in Bedford Thompson's new tasting room in historic Los Alamos.

448 Bell Street, Los Alamos | 805/344-2107 | bedfordthompsonwinery.com

16 | STOLPMAN

Take a break from Solvang's windmills and such in Stolpman's in-town tasting room. The winery has become a leading producer of Syrah here, but its Bordeaux blend, called Limestone Hill Cuvée, is also superb.

**1659 Copenhagen Drive, Suite C, Solvang | 805/688-0400 |
stolpmanvineyards.com**

FAVORITES & DISCOVERIES ☆ SANTA YNEZ

FESS PARKER WINERY & VINEYARDS *Dependable everyday drinking wine, with a tourist-friendly tasting room and store*

ZACA MESA WINERY & VINEYARD *Where some of the area's most famous winemakers learned their craft*

ANDREW MURRAY VINEYARDS *Longtime valley grower's winery and the Syrah that's produced there are worth seeking out*

STOLPMAN *Represents a new generation of winemakers giving travelers a reason to visit Solvang besides Danish pastry*

SANTA RITA WINERIES

17 | MOSBY WINERY & VINEYARDS

Practically the first winery you come to from Highway 101, Mosby is unlike any other in the Santa Rita Hills—devoted to Italian grapes (many), in some good and some not-so-good renditions. But the rustic compound is always an interesting stop.

9496 Santa Rosa Road, Buellton | 800/706-6729 | mosbywines.com

18 | ALMA ROSA WINERY & VINEYARDS

Richard Sanford—divorced from his namesake winery—has launched yet another: Alma Rosa, in the Santa Rita Hills, with certified organic vineyards and green practices in general. While he's also making Chardonnay and Pinot Gris, as well as a couple of other wines (all closed with screw caps), Pinot Noir is the real story, as it should be from this Pinot pioneer. The one from his Encantada Vineyard is beautiful.

7250 Santa Rosa Road, Buellton | 805/688-9090 | almarosawinery.com

19 | LAFOND WINERY AND VINEYARDS

This stylish tasting room and winery run by some of the area's wine pioneers is home to interesting Pinot Noirs, Chardonnays, and Syrahs. The patio turns into a crush pad during harvest, but when it's quiet, it's a great place to enjoy some wine.

6855 Santa Rosa Road, Buellton | 805/688-7921 | lafondwinery.com

20 | SANFORD WINERY

The winery that Richard Sanford founded (it's now a part of the Terlato Wine Group) has moved west into a new tasting room at La Rinconada, home of the Sanford Winery itself and 160 acres of Pinot Noir and Chardonnay vineyards. In a nod, perhaps, to the old, rustic Sanford tasting room, this new one is made of recycled timbers salvaged from an old barn.

5010 Santa Rosa Road, Lompoc | 805/688-3300 | sanfordwinery.com

21 | FOLEY ESTATES VINEYARD & WINERY

One of the newest and sleekest facilities in the Santa Rita Hills is a place to taste yummy, showcase Pinots from the region, with great views of the hills themselves and vineyards that take advantage of them. A few years ago, Foley split from its homey sister winery in the Santa Ynez Valley, Lincourt, to take Pinot to new heights.

6121 East Highway 246, Lompoc | 805/737-6222 | foleywines.com

22 | MELVILLE VINEYARDS AND WINERY

Brothers Chad and Brent Melville, with über-winemaker Greg Brewer of Brewer-Clifton, are making very impressive Pinot Noirs in this Mediterranean villa–like winery with rotunda, courtyard, and surrounding sycamores. The Syrah is worth seeking out too.

5185 East Highway 246, Lompoc | 805/735-7030 | melvillevineyards.com

23 | BABCOCK WINERY & VINEYARDS

In the 1980s, Bryan Babcock was named one of the Top Ten Small Production Winemakers in the World by the James Beard Foundation. With a new winemaker, the winery continues the tradition today with reliably good Chardonnay and Pinot Noir.

5175 East Highway 246, Lompoc | 805/736-1455 | babcockwinery.com

24 | CLOS PEPE VINEYARDS AND ESTATE WINES

Clos Pepe (pronounced "peppy") Vineyards is a source for some better-known wine-making names in the area—Hitching Post, Siduri, Brewer-Clifton—but they also make a small amount of Pinot and even smaller amount of Chardonnay under their own label. The vineyard manager, Wes Hagen, is the winemaker, and his wife, Chanda, is assistant winemaker.

4777 East Highway 246, Lompoc | 805/735-2196 (call for appointment) | clospepe.com

25 | FIDDLEHEAD CELLARS

Winemaker-owner Kathy Joseph brings a generous spirit and great Pinot Noir (from her Fiddlestix Vineyard) to the Santa Rita Hills. She makes some Pinot from Oregon grapes too, so interesting comparisons arise. The winery is in the up-and-coming Lompoc Wine Ghetto, an industrial area behind the Home Depot at Highways 1 and 246. (Sea Smoke and Brewer-Clifton also call the Ghetto home, but neither are open to the public.)

1597 East Chestnut Avenue, Lompoc | 800/251-1225 | fiddleheadcellars.com

26 | PALMINA

After stopping in at Fiddlehead, visit Palmina. Run by Brewer-Clifton partner Steve Clifton and his wife, Chrystal, Palmina brings a splash of Italy to the Central Coast. Palmina produces two Pinot Grigios: one from its Honea Vineyard in the Santa Ynez Valley and another from its Alisos Vineyard in Los Alamos.

1520 East Chestnut Court, Lompoc | 805/735-2030 | palminawines.com

FAVORITES & DISCOVERIES ☆ SANTA RITA HILLS

ALMA ROSA WINERY & VINEYARDS *Pinot pioneer Richard Sanford has come home with the opening of his new winery*

SANFORD WINERY *A new tasting room gets visitors closer to where the winery's famous Pinot Noir and Chardonnay grapes grow*

MELVILLE VINEYARDS AND WINERY *Melville has played a big part in putting the Santa Rita Hills on the map*

FIDDLEHEAD CELLARS *Located in the nascent Lompoc Wine Ghetto, it's devoted to Sauvignon Blanc and Pinot Noir*

SANTA MARIA WINERIES

I | COSTA DE ORO

The Gold Coast Marketplace in Santa Maria is a new venue for wine, fresh produce, and other gourmet foods. Costa de Oro wines from winemaker Gary Burk share space here with yummy goods from Gold Coast Farms.

1331 South Nicholson Avenue (Highway 101 at Stowell Road), Santa Maria | 805/922-1468 | costadeorowinery.com

2 | COTTONWOOD CANYON VINEYARD & WINERY

A bright, airy, friendly space to taste Santa Maria Valley wines. Cottonwood's vineyards, which were planted in north-south rows to soak up as much sun as possible when the Beko family purchased the estate in 1988, contain equal parts Pinot Noir and Chardonnay, with a smaller 5-acre parcel devoted to Syrah.

3940 Dominion Road, Santa Maria | 805/937-8463 | cottonwoodcanyon.com

3 | CAMBRIA

Owned by Barbara Banke and husband Jess Jackson of Northern California's Kendall-Jackson empire, Cambria has the air of a place ready for tour buses. But the signature Julia's Vineyard Pinot Noir is good; in fact, Pinot comparisons here are fascinating.

5475 Chardonnay Lane, Santa Maria | 888/339-9463 | cambriawines.com

4 | BYRON

A modern facility given to experimenting in the vineyard with dense plantings and vertical trellises, Byron was founded by former Zaca Mesa winemaker Ken Brown, owned for a while by Robert Mondavi, and is now part of Jackson Family Farms. Through

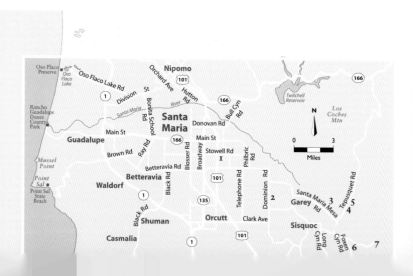

SPOTLIGHT PINOT NOIR

Pinot Noir has inspired more lurid prose than a history of sunsets. It "wraps you in silk pajamas" and offers up flavors of "strawberries, blueberries, dried cherries, rose petals, green tea, licorice, black pepper, cola, vanilla, mushrooms, cedar, pipe-tobacco smoke, sweaty leather …" Sweaty leather? ☆ Good Pinot Noir is an exquisite alternative to the pounding tannins of Cabernet Sauvignon and a terrific complement to both white- and red-leaning foods. But making wine from Pinot grapes is like having a high-maintenance friend. Thin-skinned, sensitive to conditions, and susceptible to mildew, Pinot needs leaf-by-leaf and berry-by-berry attention in the vineyard. In the winery, while sturdy Cab is being generally beaten into cleanliness and submission, moody, volatile Pinot requires the gentlest hand. There are enough caveats on the way to great Pinot to drive a sane man crazy—and a rebel to make Pinot Noir.

all these changes, the winemaking has remained true to Brown's original vision, with great results. The overlook from the winery's front patio is as rich as its Pinot Noir.

**5250 Tepusquet Road, Santa Maria |
805/934-4770, ext. 11 (call for appointment) | byronwines.com**

5 | KENNETH VOLK VINEYARDS

Ken Volk built Wild Horse in Paso Robles from a 600-case-a-year start-up to a 150,000-case-a-year giant, sold it to a subsidiary of Jim Beam Brands, wrested the original Byron property from Robert Mondavi Winery, and has started all over again. If you followed that, you haven't been drinking enough of his Santa Maria Chardonnay and Pinot.

5230 Tepusquet Road, Santa Maria | 805/938-7896 | volkwines.com

6 | FOXEN WINERY & VINEYARD

This farm-hut tasting room is beyond rustic, but Foxen produces good Pinot Noirs and Chardonnays, even better Syrahs, and a Cabernet Franc.

7200 Foxen Canyon Road, Santa Maria | 805/937-4251 | foxenvineyard.com

7 | RANCHO SISQUOC

One of the most picturesque places to taste wine in the Santa Maria Valley. Steve Clifton of Brewer-Clifton got his start here. Try the Cellar Select Meritage.

6600 Foxen Canyon Road, Santa Maria | 805/934-4332 | ranchosisquoc.com

THINGS TO DO

LA PURISIMA MISSION STATE PARK

Many California mission fans list this among their very favorites, for its gorgeous setting and the substantial archaeology work that has taken place here.

2295 Purisima Road, Lompoc | **805/733-3713** | **lapurisimamission.org**

LOMPOC FLOWER FIELDS

Flowers grown for the cut-flower market and for seed bloom from June through August just east of town. Look for sweet peas, delphiniums, larkspur, and sunflowers off North Bailey Avenue—and the roads that parallel it to the east—between West Central Avenue and Highway 246.

805/736-4567 | **lompoc.com**

LOTUSLAND

South of Santa Barbara, in Montecito, sits the 37-acre estate known as Lotusland, which has been a showcase for plants since the 1880s when it was the home of a local nurseryman. The gardens include a citrus orchard, a world-class collection of cycads, and an impressive army of cactus. You can visit from mid-February through mid-November, by reservation only.

695 Ashley Road, Santa Barbara | **805/969-9990** | **lotusland.org**

OLD MISSION SANTA INÉS

On the edge of Solvang, this lovely mission has fine views of the Santa Ynez Valley.

1760 Mission Drive, Solvang | **805/688-4815** | **missionsantaines.org**

PACIFIC CONSERVATORY OF THE PERFORMING ARTS

The PCPA is one of the best repertory companies on the West Coast, and its outdoor theater in downtown Solvang is a gem.

420 Second Street, Solvang | **805/922-8313** | **pcpa.org**

SANTA BARBARA COUNTY COURTHOUSE

The extensive tile work and intricately painted ceilings and beams inside are breathtaking, as are the views of red-roofed Santa Barbara outside.

1100 Anacapa Street, Santa Barbara | **805/962-6464** | **santabarbaracourthouse.org**

SANTA YNEZ VALLEY MUSEUM/PARKS JANEWAY CARRIAGE HOUSE

Boasts the largest collection of restored stagecoaches west of the Mississippi.

Sagunto and Faraday streets, Santa Ynez | **805/688-7889** | **syvm.org**

WHALE WATCHING

It used to be that whale watching in the Santa Barbara Channel was a winter-to-spring affair, as gray whales migrated south and north respectively. But since the 1990s, large pods of blues and humpbacks have been common every summer, which has prompted tour operators to offer warm-weather excursions. One of the most comfortable ways to see cetaceans is aboard the Condor Express.

301 West Cabrillo Boulevard, Santa Barbara | 888/779-4253 | condorcruises.com

WILDLING ART MUSEUM

A must-see, excellent museum that focuses on art inspired by American nature.

2329 Jonata Street, Los Olivos | 805/688-1082 | wildlingmuseum.org

SPOTLIGHT SANTA BARBARA

To visit Santa Barbara's wine country without exploring the city of Santa Barbara is a little like wine tasting in Tuscany without ever setting foot in Florence. Thirty minutes from the Santa Ynez Valley's vineyards lies one of the most beautiful cities in the world: a mix of beach town and upper-class retreat, where money old and new mixes with surfers, scientists, artists, and University of California students. ☆ The ideal Santa Barbara visit samples all the city's facets: historic, luxurious, athletic. In a city of notable Spanish-style architecture, **Mission Santa Barbara** (2201 Laguna Street; 805/682-4149; sbmission.org) is the most impressive of all. Self-guided tours daily from 9 to 5. ☆ The true soul of the city lies along the water. At East Beach, artists set up easels while volleyball players set and spike. At the harbor, the **Ty Warner Sea Center** (211 Stearns Wharf; 805/962-2526; sbnature.org) on historic Stearns Wharf celebrates the marine environment. **Santa Barbara Maritime Museum** (113 Harbor Way; 805/962-8404; sbmm.org) is another fine harborside museum. Join a catamaran cruise or rent a kayak at the **Santa Barbara Sailing Center** (Santa Barbara Harbor Boat Launch; 805/962-2826; sbsail.com). Head out into the Santa Barbara Channel and look back. Here's the red-tiled city, spread between mountains and sea, looking like a movie set, but perfectly real.

WHERE TO EAT

BOUCHON

Tucked just off of State Street, an intimate charmer that features local produce and Santa Barbara County wines.

9 West Victoria Street, Santa Barbara | 805/730-1160 | bouchonsantabarbara.com

BROTHERS' RESTAURANT AT MATTEI'S TAVERN

This longtime local landmark has lately blossomed into one of the best dining destinations in the area. The brothers responsible for this transformation are Jeff and Matt Nichols, who have worked with Rick Bayless and Wolfgang Puck.

2350 Railway Avenue, Los Olivos | 805/688-4820 | matteistavern.com

CAFE ANGELICA

In Danish downtown Solvang, a charming restaurant with a pretty patio and a sure touch with steaks, salmon, and pasta.

490 First Street, Solvang | 805/686-9970

SPOTLIGHT SANTA MARIA BARBECUE

*Maybe it's just coincidence that Santa Barbara County produces great big red wines that go particularly well with barbecue. Or maybe it's some kind of cosmic harmonic beef-and-grape convergence. ☆ The fact is that along with its wines, the region's biggest claim to gastronomic fame is that it's the home to Santa Maria Barbecue. Which is to say, the locally favored cut of tri-tip seasoned with salt and pepper and garlic, then grilled over a red oak fire to produce some of the best damn barbecue you've ever had. Classic accompaniments are salsa, pinquito beans, and garlic bread—and, of course, that red wine. ☆ On most Friday nights and Saturdays Santa Maria civic organizations set up their grills along Broadway and Main and sell barbecue to the hungry waiting world. Tip-top tri-tip venues include The Hitching Post II's sibling, **The Hitching Post** (3325 Point Sal Road, Casmalia; 805/937-6151; hitchingpost1.com), **The Far Western Tavern** (899 Guadalupe Street, Guadalupe; 805/343-2211), **Jocko's Steak House** (125 North Thompson Street, Nipomo; 805/929-3686), and **Shaw's Steak House** (714 South Broadway, Santa Maria; 805/925-5862).*

COLD SPRING TAVERN

A satisfying detour since 1886, when the first stagecoach stopped here. Breakfasts on the weekends include venison sausage patties; burgers are good anytime.

5995 Stagecoach Road, Santa Barbara | 805/967-0066 | coldspringtavern.com

DOWNEY'S

This award-winning French-California favorite is conveniently located downtown. The wine list features bottles by Au Bon Climat, Qupé, and Williams Selyem.

1305 State Street, Santa Barbara | 805/966-5006 | downeyssb.com

THE HITCHING POST II

A convivial, family-friendly place that just happens to offer some of the best steaks in California and potent Pinot Noirs produced by restaurant-owner Frank Ostini and his partner Gray Hartley.

406 East Highway 246, Buellton | 805/688-0676 | hitchingpost2.com

LA SUPER-RICA TAQUERIA

No pretenses, just great Mexican food at picnic tables beneath a plastic awning.

622 North Milpas Street, Santa Barbara | 805/963-4940

LOS OLIVOS CAFÉ

Scene of a famously bibulous dinner in *Sideways,* the cafe serves California-Mediterranean cuisine in an airy cottage settings.

2879 Grand Avenue, Los Olivos | 805/688-7265 | losolivoscafe.com

OLIO E LIMONE

Italian fare rules next door to very French Bouchon. Order a bottle of Alban Viognier to accompany your risotto with shrimp, asparagus, lemon, and chives.

11 West Victoria, Suite 17, Santa Barbara | 805/899-2699 | olioelimone.com

PATRICK'S SIDE STREET CAFÉ

Excellent salads and sandwiches for lunch; beef and seafood for dinner.

2375 Alamo Pintado Road, Los Olivos | 805/686-4004 | patrickssidestreetcafe.com

WINE CASK RESTAURANT

In downtown's historic El Prado, an elegant restaurant with a superb wine list.

13 Anacapa Street, Santa Barbara | 805/966-9463 | winecask.com

PLACES TO STAY

ALISAL GUEST RANCH AND RESORT

Beautiful 10,000-acre guest ranch still has its own cattle herd, not to mention two 18-hole golf courses, fly-fishing, and seemingly infinite horseback riding opportunities. 73 suites from $450 (meals and activities included). Two-night minimum.

1054 Alisal Road, Solvang | **888/425-4725** | **alisal.com**

BALLARD INN & RESTAURANT

In a leafy little hamlet famous for its one-room schoolhouse, a luxurious country inn with a first-rate restaurant. 15 rooms from $215.

2436 Baseline Avenue, Ballard | **800/638-2466** | **ballardinn.com**

BRISAS DEL MAR, INN AT THE BEACH

Two blocks from the beach, it's modeled after a Mediterranean villa; some suites have hot tubs and kitchens. 31 rooms from $154.

223 Castillo Street, Santa Barbara | **800/468-1988** | **sbhotels.com**

EL CAPITAN CANYON

El Capitán and Refugio State Beaches are terrific places for kayaking. Camp at either (visit reserveamerica.com) or stay in a cedar cabin at El Capitan Canyon on the other side Highway 101. 108 cabins from $185, 26 tents from $135.

11560 Calle Real, Santa Barbara | **866/352-2729** | **elcapitancanyon.com**

FESS PARKER'S WINE COUNTRY INN & SPA VIGNE

Lavish small resort on Los Olivos's gallery-lined Grand Avenue. Across the street, its Spa Vigne offers massages and facials to help you recover from that long hard day of tasting Pinots. 21 rooms from $280.

2860 Grand Avenue, Los Olivos | **800/446-2455** | **fessparker.com**

FOUR SEASONS RESORT SANTA BARBARA

A splurge, but worth it for the resort's oceanside setting, gardens, and graceful Spanish architecture. 207 rooms from $500.

1260 Channel Drive, Santa Barbara | **888/424-5866** | **fourseasons.com/santabarbara**

HOTEL OCEANA

Ask about the Oceans to Vineyards package, which includes a Jeep tour to four local wineries. 63 suites from $335.

202 West Cabrillo Boulevard, Santa Barbara | **800/777-9758** | **hoteloceanasantabarbara.com**

SANTA BARBARA INN

Prime location across from the East Beach volleyball courts. 69 rooms from $209.

**901 East Cabrillo Boulevard, Santa Barbara | 800/231-0431 |
santabarbarainn.com**

SANTA YNEZ INN

Neo-Victorian splendor in downtown Santa Ynez. 14 rooms from $285.

**3627 Sagunto Street, Santa Ynez | 800/643-5774 |
santaynezinn.com**

VILLA ROSA

A Spanish Colonial inn with a lovely courtyard, and it's just a short stroll from East Beach. In winter months, splurge on a room with a fireplace. 18 rooms from $149.

**15 Chapala Street, Santa Barbara | 805/966-0851 |
villarosainnsb.com**

SPOTLIGHT SAN YSIDRO RANCH

*Santa Barbara has no shortage of luxe places to stay, but in terms of history and star power, the San Ysidro Ranch (900 San Ysidro Lane, Santa Barbara; 800/368-6788; sanysidro ranch.com) is in a class by itself. ☆ Set on a wooded hillside above Montecito, wealthy Santa Barbara's even wealthier suburb, the Ranch is where John and Jackie Kennedy honeymooned and Oprah staged her 50th birthday party. San Ysidro acquired its Hollywood cachet in the 1930s, when actor Ronald Coleman turned the 1893 property into a getaway for film friends like Cary Grant, Gloria Swanson, and Sir Laurence. What these notables found—what you still find today—is a resort that manages to be both supremely posh and unpretentious. Thirty-two cottages are set among lush gardens, offering both luxury and the kind of privacy you need when People paparazzi are clamoring to get a photo of your newly adopted baby. There are the requisite tennis courts, a swimming pool, and trails leading into the surrounding mountains, all starting at just $800 a night (paradise has never come cheap). Short of spending the night, you can get a taste of the place by dining at either of the Ranch's two good restaurants, **The Stonehouse Inn** and the more informal **Plow and Angel Bistro**.*

TEMECULA

TRAVELING EAST ON RANCHO CALIFORNIA ROAD in Temecula, you come to Hart Winery just after the road narrows from four lanes to two. Since Hart opened in 1980, subdivisions have crept to within a quarter mile of its western edge, but, as owner Joe Hart explains, "The houses are going to stay *there*. This," he says of his vineyard in Temecula Valley's wine country, "is zoned long-term for agriculture."

Grapes have earned a valuable place here in the rolling hills of southwestern Riverside County. And they deserve it. The vintners in Temecula Valley are making wines of impressive sophistication. Even better: The area is just an hour from San Diego and 90 minutes from Los Angeles, making Temecula the easiest wine country for Southern Californians and visitors to explore. A loop drive on Rancho California Road and other back roads east of Temecula leads to 21 wineries.

Joe Hart's winery is a good place to start. Its Syrah is a fine example of the full-bodied reds being made in Temecula and typifies what Hart calls an "ABC winery: anything but Chardonnay."

Not that you'd have to look far for Chardonnay. Next door to Hart, Callaway Coastal Winery started here in 1969 and made a name for itself in the '80s with its all-white lineup, much of it Chardonnay. Callaway's large tasting room continues to draw big crowds. So, too, does its restaurant, Allie's at Callaway, which occupies a series of covered terraced patios that overlooks a vine-covered hillside.

Besides Callaway, three other Temecula wineries have restaurants on their premises—Baily Vineyard & Winery, Ponte Family Estate, and Thornton Winery, which is notable for its sparkling wine. About seven kinds are produced at the château-like facility.

Temecula Valley's southerly location has worked against the notion that it could produce quality wines. Many people, Hart says, "had the impression that we were in the desert. But then they came down here and tasted Temecula Riesling, and they said, 'Gee, it's really good.'"

True, Temecula is California's southernmost wine country, but it's just 25 miles from the Pacific Ocean, at an elevation of 1,500 feet. Days are warm and nights are cool, a combination that—along with the well-drained soil—can support many varieties typically grown farther north, including Gewürztraminer, Merlot, and Sauvignon Blanc.

And Temecula's latitude can also be an advantage. "We in Temecula are uniquely suited to produce warm-climate varieties," says Etienne Cowper, winemaker at Mount Palomar Winery, which introduced Cortese, Sangiovese, and Syrah to Temecula.

If winemaking is serious in Temecula, wine tasting is, for the most part, Southern California casual. At the family-run Wilson Creek Winery, the easternmost winery on Rancho California, manager Bill Wilson eschews the idea that wine tasting has to be stuffy. "I think the best wine is the one you like," he says. Weekends find Wilson Creek's tasting room and patio brimming with visitors. Many of the first-timers may have heard about the very popular almond-infused sparkling wine. But varieties like the Estate Zinfandel will give them a new appreciation for the winemaking taking place in Southern California's backyard.

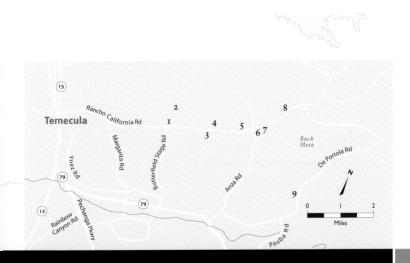

WINERIES

1 | HART WINERY

The old-school tasting room is small and unadorned, but it's a must-stop for lovers of Cab, Merlot, and Mediterranean reds like Syrah and Tempranillo.

41300 Avenida Biona, Temecula | 951/676-6300 | thehartfamilywinery.com

2 | BAILY VINEYARD & WINERY

Red Bordeaux varietals—Cab, Merlot, Cab Franc—are the best bets here, along with the very good Meritage made from them. Whites include a Sauvignon Blanc–Semillion blend. Carol's Restaurant, on site, serves lunch inside and (weather permitting) out.

33440 La Serena Way, Temecula | 951/676-9463 | bailywinery.com

3 | THORNTON WINERY

Notable for its bubbly (usually about six kinds), but produces many good still wines too. Tasting is a sit-down affair, offered in flights. Weekend jazz concerts April through October are held on the large Mediterranean-style terrace.

32575 Rancho California Road, Temecula | 951/699-0099 | thorntonwine.com

4 | CALLAWAY VINEYARD & WINERY

Founded by Ely Callaway, who went on to change the world of golf equipment, Callaway is one of Temecula's biggest wineries. With a large tasting room that offers views of vineyards in almost every direction, Callaway makes wine to suit a range of tastes.

32720 Rancho California Road, Temecula | 951/676-4001 | callawaywinery.com

5 | MOUNT PALOMAR WINERY

Its tasting room isn't as grand as those of some of its newer neighbors, but Mount Palomar is one of Temecula's must-visit wineries, with a Sangiovese that shines year after year, an excellent medium-dry Riesling, and a cream sherry that has won many converts. In all, 16 varieties of grapes grow in its 40-acre vineyard.

33820 Rancho California Road, Temecula | 951/676-5047 | mountpalomar.com

6 | SOUTH COAST WINERY RESORT & SPA

Temecula's largest winery facility has a sizable tasting room, the Vineyard Rose restaurant, guest villas, a full-service day spa, even a conference facility. Of its wide range of wines, those from Wild Horse Peak Mountain Vineyards have the most gusto.

34843 Rancho California Road, Temecula | 951/587-9463 | wineresort.com

7 | PONTE FAMILY ESTATE

Although the winery opened in 2003, the Ponte brothers have been growing grapes in Temecula since 1984. Their experience shows in the Nebbiolo and the Super Tuscan blend. Pleasant grounds and the Smokehouse restaurant in back.

35053 Rancho California Road, Temecula | 951/694-8855 | pontewinery.com

8 | WILSON CREEK WINERY

A good-time vibe draws a youngish crowd to Wilson Creek, especially in summer. The Estate Zinfandel is the unsung hero here.

35960 Rancho California Road, Temecula | 951/699-9463 | wilsoncreekwinery.com

9 | LEONESSE CELLARS

With its high-ceilinged, somewhat formal tasting room inside a Tudor-style building, Leonesse, founded in 2003, feels more Napa than SoCal. Nice views of vineyards and Temecula Valley's less-developed east side. Don't miss the Cinsault Port.

38311 De Portola Road, Temecula | 951/302-7601 | leonessecellars.com

PLACES TO STAY

EMBASSY SUITES HOTEL TEMECULA VALLEY WINE COUNTRY

Close to the center of the city of Temecula. 136 rooms from $149.

29345 Rancho California Road, Temecula | 951/676-5656 | embassysuites.com/es/temecula

LOMA VISTA BED & BREAKFAST

In the heart of the wine country, this simple but comfortable B&B overlooks a hill planted with citrus trees. 10 rooms from $120.

33350 La Serena Way, Temecula | 951/676-7047 | lomavistabb.com

PECHANGA RESORT & CASINO

Tastefully appointed rooms and casino atmosphere. 522 rooms from $99.

45000 Pechanga Parkway, Temecula | 877/711-2946 | pechanga.com

TEMECULA CREEK INN

Features a 27-hole championship golf course. 129 rooms from $149.

44501 Rainbow Canyon Road, Temecula | 800/962-7335 | temeculacreekinn.com

THERE'S BEEN WINEMAKING IN MEXICO since before California vintners could say "new French oak." But it wasn't until about 20 years ago that a special little valley in northern Baja California—just 90 minutes south of San Diego—began growing grapes capable of producing great wine. Now the Guadalupe Valley, which angles northeast from Ensenada, is becoming a bona fide "wine country" at an astonishing rate.

To the north, south, and east, the valley is cupped by dramatic mountain ranges, which allow ocean breezes to flow in from the west and then be held there. As a result, the area doesn't get as hot as you might expect, so the grapes can retain their all-important acid. And because the growing season is long, winemakers can count on complex, concentrated flavors.

Back in the 18th century, Spanish missionaries discovered the region's wine-related merits when they planted grapes for sacramental wine. Grapes from the Valle de Guadalupe produced better wine than those grown anywhere else in Mexico. Rather than applauding the success of its colonizers, Spain felt threatened by this new-world bounty (for good reason, it turns out—last year a Guadalupe Valley wine won in a blind tasting over its Spanish counterparts). Spain eventually forbade the mission fathers from putting their vines to commercial use, and by 1910, most of the remaining vineyards were destroyed, despite none-other-than Pancho Villa's efforts to protect a few of them.

Fast-forward about a century and everywhere you look in the Guadalupe Valley you see new vineyards and new wineries. American Don Miller and his Dutch wife, Tru, arrived in the valley in 1998 to build Adobe Guadalupe, a combination winery and bed-and-breakfast.

Continues page 152 >

SUGGESTED ROUTES

☆ **TECATE TO GUADALUPE VALLEY** Curvy, mountainous Highway 3 demands an attentive driver—even Tecate locals caution against navigating it at dusk or at night, and especially not after a day of tasting wine. If you are visiting San Diego, this is a good route to the valley because it avoids border traffic at Tijuana.

☆ **SOUTH OF ENSENADA** After mingling with the tourists in Ensenada, drive south on Highway 1 to explore the beaches of Bahia de Todos Santos. At the far end of the Punta Banda peninsula is La Bufadora, where you can rent Scuba equipment, snorkels, and kayaks.

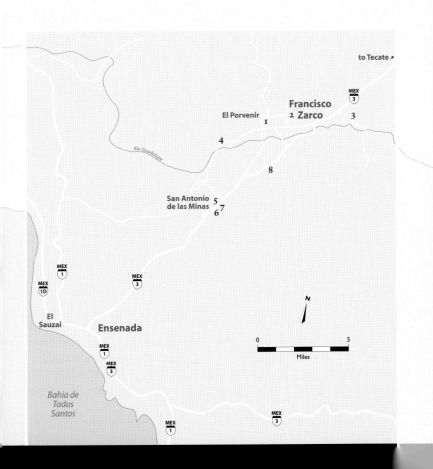

At Monte Xanic, founded in the 1980s, owner Hans Backhoff's French-trained son, Hans Joseph, has just dynamited a new cave out of the hill beneath this Greek temple–like winery.

And then there's Casa de Piedra's Hugo d'Acosta—the maker of that earthy Tempranillo-Cabernet blend that bested the Spaniards—who comes to Baja winemaking armed with a Ph.D. in enology from France's University of Montpellier and winemaking experience in both Italy and the Napa Valley. With a researcher's passion, d'Acosta is determined to find out which grapes do well in what parts of the valley, and what specific traits each area brings to the fruit. His next step in the quest to sort out this Wild West of wines, where growers have planted a muddle of varietals from Chardonnay to Nebbiolo, is to build a new winery where he'll produce separate bottlings of the same varieties grown in different parts of the valley; he's named this new experimental winery Paralelo.

A growing number of day-trippers are driving down from Southern California to tour the Guadalupe Valley, each carrying back the two bottles that U.S. Customs lets them bring home from Mexico. The Mexican government has established a Ruta del Vino that runs among the vineyards, although much of it is washboard rough.

And word is getting out within Mexico, even though the entire population of the country drinks less wine in a year than the city of San Diego alone. High-end restaurants in Mexico City used to favor mainly French wines. But not long ago, Tru and Don Miller sat down to dinner with Hugo d'Acosta in a swank Mexico City dining spot. They saw one of d'Acosta's wines on the wine list. It was going for $125.

The priests, and Pancho Villa, would be proud.

WINERIES

1 | ADOBE GUADALUPE

Enjoy exciting wine blends at the granite tasting bar in the winery's tower—when was the last time you tasted a wine made from Cabernet Franc, Tempranillo, Grenache, Chenin Blanc, Moscatel, *and* Viognier?

**3 miles south of Francisco Zarco in El Porvenir |
011-52-646-155-2094 (call for appointment) | adobeguadalupe.com**

2 | MONTE XANIC

This winery secured the valley's reputation in the 1980s and now has a dramatic new cave. The Gran Ricardo, sold only by the magnum, is bottle aged for four years.

**2 miles south of Francisco Zarco |
011-52-646-174-6155 (call for appointment) | montexanic.com**

3 | L.A. CETTO

The biggest producer in Mexico, it's the only winery we are aware of with a bullfighting ring as well as a tasting room.

Highway 3 at km 73.5 | 011-52-646-155-2264 | lacetto.com

4 | BIBAYOFF

As its name suggests, this winery's heritage is Russian. As for Bibayoff's wines, they are often eccentric—a Cabernet-Zinfandel-Port is not something you see every day.

**3 miles south of El Porvenir in Toros Pintos |
011-52-646-176-1008 (call for appointment)**

5 | CASA DE PIEDRA

Hugo d'Acosta pours a stunning unoaked Chardonnay at his picturesque winery, which is a stone farmhouse outside, cutting-edge inside.

**Highway 3 at km 93.5 |
011-52-646-156-5268 (call for appointment) | vinoscasadepiedra.com**

6 | VINISTERRA

The founder's grandfather—General Abelardo Rodriguez, then governor of Baja California and later president of Mexico—bought the area's first winery in the 1930s and brought an experienced Italian winemaker to the region.

**Highway 3 near km 93 |
011-52-646-178-3350 (call for appointment) | vinisterra.com**

7 | VIÑA DE LICEAGA

The family-owned winery in San Antonio de las Minas makes two Merlots and bottles the only grappa made in Mexico.

Highway 3 at km 93 | 011-52-646-178-2922 | vinosliceaga.com

9 | MOGOR-BADAN

Its owner is an oceanographer who moonlights as the winemaker here—he produces less than 500 cases a year.

Highway 3 at km 86.5 | 011-52-646-171-1484 (call for appointment)

THINGS TO DO

ENSENADA

There's a reason why so many cruise ships stop at Ensenada—most of the sights passengers want to see are just a short walk from the docks. One of their first stops is also one of the best, the Riviera del Pacifico Cultural Center, which was built as a casino in 1920s and reputedly financed by Al Capone. Then it's on to a gauntlet of shopping along Avenida Lopez Mateos. At the western end of the boulevard, at Ruiz, is Hussong's Cantina, the place where the margarita was born.

enjoyensenada.com

BAHIA DE TODOS SANTOS

For a break from urban Ensenada, explore the beaches along the bay. Though something of a tourist trap, La Bufadora, at the end of the Punta Banda peninsula, is a good place to Scuba, snorkel, kayak, or just follow the crowds to admire the eponymous blowhole. You can rent all sorts of gear at Dave's Dive Shop.

011-52-646-154-2092 | labufadoradive.com

GOLF

Numerous golf courses with spectacular ocean views can be found between Tijuana and Ensenada. A good choice near Tijuana is the course at Real Del Mar, where you can play 18 holes midweek for $69. Just north of Ensenada is Bajamar, where 18 holes during the week at twilight run just $35.

Real Del Mar, 800/803-6038 | realdelmar.com.mx
Bajamar, 619/425-0081 | bajamar.com

WHALE WATCHING

Beginning in late December and continuing through March, gray whales arrive off the coast of Baja after feeding all summer in the Bering Sea. Numerous Ensenada boat operators offer whale-watching trips into Bahia de Todos Santos, including Sergio's Sportfishing Center and Marina.

800/336-5454 (weekdays), 011-52-646-178-2185 |
sergios-sportfishing.com

WHERE TO EAT

RESTAURANT LAJA

The best (and only great) restaurant in the valley, with sophisticated fixed-price meals, Restaurant Laja alone is worth a drive from Tecate or Ensenada.

Highway 3 at km 83 | 011-52-646-155-2556 | lajamexico.com

PLACES TO STAY

ADOBE GUADALUPE

Horseback riding through the vineyards and huevos rancheros for breakfast are among the features at this high-end Spanish-style B&B. 6 rooms from $168.

3 miles south of Francisco Zarco in El Porvenir | 011-52-646-155-2094 | adobeguadalupe.com

LAS BRISAS DEL VALLE

Beautiful views of the Guadalupe Valley, a spa and a swimming pool, and cuisine prepared with organic produce. 6 rooms from $150.

Highway 3 at km 89 | 011-52-646-113-3629 | lasbrisasdelvalle.com

ESTERO BEACH HOTEL RESORT

This family-friendly resort south of Ensenada offers horseback riding on the beach, bike rentals, and bookings with area sportfishing operators. 100 rooms from $60.

011-52-646-176-6225 | hotelesterobeach.com

SPOTLIGHT RANCHO LA PUERTA

Rancho La Puerta is a 3,000-acre, self-contained oasis in Tecate, which means most guests are content to stay put upon their arrival to take classes designed to improve the mind, spirit, and body; to hike to the top of nearby Mount Kuchumaa; and to dine on the ranch's lacto-ovo vegetarian cuisine, which is as delicious as it is good for you. ☆ In recent years, Rancho La Puerta has begun cultivating its connection to the burgeoning wine country that lies only about an hour by car to the south. Some guests use Rancho La Puerta as a base from which to visit Baja's wineries, if only for an afternoon. Others deliberately book their stays during the ranch's two special culinary weeks a year—a guided tour of the wineries in the Guadalupe Valley is offered, and lunch or dinner at **Restaurant Laja** is often on the itinerary. For those who prefer their Rancho La Puerta experience to be uninterrupted, ranch staffers can help them coordinate visits to the Guadalupe Valley either prior to or after their stay. ☆ From $2,535 per week, per person (program and meals included); 800/443-7565; rancholapuerta.com

GLOSSARY

Acidity Acids occur naturally in wine and are one of the components that keep wine balanced as it ages. Generally, the riper the grapes, the higher the sugar levels and the lower the acidity. In recent years there's been a trend toward higher sugar levels in wines, but some winemakers have resisted this trend since low acidity can produce wines that taste flat or lifeless.

Appellation and AVA In the United States, the word appellation is often used, somewhat imprecisely, to refer to the official American Viticultural Area, or AVA, where the grapes for a particular wine are grown, bottled, or both. Some appellations, Napa for example, contain many smaller AVAs within them.

Barrel-fermented Fermentation is the process that converts the naturally occurring sugars in wine to alcohol. White wines are often fermented in oak barrels to give their flavor a creamier, less-fruity quality.

Blend Any wine made from different varieties of grapes, the same variety of grapes from different vineyards, or grapes whose fermentation methods vary (for example, a Chardonnay that is not 100 percent barrel-fermented) is a blend.

Body This term describes the way the wine feels, in terms of its lightness or heaviness, in your mouth. Most Cabernet Sauvignons have more body than your typical Pinot Noirs.

Bottle aging After a wine has been bottled, it is sometimes left to age for up to several years before it is released for sale. As wine ages, the up-front fruit flavors mellow and fade, and the under-lying secondary flavors come to the fore, so wines that are bottle aged tend to be more complex than ones that are not.

Brix Prior to harvest, a winemaker will measure the sugar content of grapes, known as the brix, to help predict the alcohol content of the wine.

Buttery Wines that are described as buttery have usually gone through malolactic fermentation, which converts one type of acid (malic) into another (lactic). The result is a wine that feels soft, or buttery, in the mouth.

Chewy This term describes wines such as Zinfandel and Syrah that have a lot of texture, as well as wines like Cabernet Sauvignon.

Corked A wine that has a nasty, musty smell when opened is described as corked. Bacteria grows naturally in cork, which is why alternative closures like screw caps are getting more atten-tion from the wine industry.

Crush To crush a grape is to literally puncture its skin so that it ferments, but crush is more often used as a noun to refer to the time of year (fall) when grapes are harvested.

Dry Wines that are low in sugar are dry. Dry wines can be fruity but they won't be especially sweet.

Estate bottled Ironically, a wine that is estate bottled is not necessarily made entirely from grapes grown on a single estate or vineyard. The phrase can also refer to a wine that is made from grapes grown within a particular AVA if the winery is in the same AVA.

Finish This word refers to the way the taste of a wine lingers, or doesn't, in your mouth after you've had a sip.

Flight Many tasting rooms offer flights, which simply means selections of wines in small samples, so that you can compare a number of wines without committing to a full glass of each.

Legs In the movies, the cliché wine-snob character will swirl his wine around in the base of a glass, lift it to his lips, sip, set the glass down, smile approvingly, and pronounce "Nice legs" in admiration of the little streams of wine that are slowly dripping down the inside of the glass. In fact, a glass of wine's legs have just about nothing to do with the quality of the wine inside the glass.

Library This is another winery-centric term that describes wines that are no longer available for sale at retail outlets. Think of library wine as the good stuff from the back room.

Meritage Meritage (rhymes with heritage) is a marketing term for U.S. wines made entirely from grapes grown in Bordeaux. Lots of wines meet this criteria, but few wineries choose to pay the modest fee required to put the word on their labels.

Nose It means pretty much what you think it means, namely, the wine's aroma (smells resulting from grape characteristics) and bouquet (smells resulting from winemaking).

Oaky Wine that's been barrel-fermented and/or aged in oak barrels sometimes has a woody, vanilla-like flavor that's described as oaky. New oak barrels produce an oakier character than older ("neutral") oak barrels.

Racking Fermentation creates sediments, so winemakers periodically siphon their fermenting wines into clean barrels, leaving sediments behind.

Riddling Turning and tilting bottles of sparkling wines so that yeast sediments settle in the bottles' necks.

Tannin If a young Cabernet makes your mouth pucker, it's probably high in tannin, which is a compound that comes from the seeds, stems, and skins of grapes. Tannin is one of the elements that permits red wines to age so well.

Terroir The sum total of environmental factors that contribute to the character of grapes in a particular vineyard, from sun and fog to soil and slope.

Varietal A wine made from at least 75 percent of a single variety of grape.

Vertical A vertical is a tasting of the same wine from consecutive years.

Vintage Refers to the year the grapes for a wine were grown and harvested, not to the year they were bottled or distributed for sale.

WINE CLUBS

One of the most perplexing problems for the time-pressed would-be wine enthusiast is deciding which wine to try next. Wine clubs are excellent solutions for such people because they supply, on a monthly or quarterly basis, new bottles to uncork and taste, in some cases selected by panels of experts.

Wine clubs fall into two basic categories: single-winery clubs and those that ship bottles from multiple wineries.

SINGLE-WINERY CLUBS

These are the winery equivalents of music fan clubs. Members typically receive two bottles from their chosen winery every quarter. Membership usually entitles you to discounts on purchases when you're visiting the winery or ordering online; complimentary tastings at the winery; and invitations to parties and/or special events. Miljenko's Cellar Club, one of two clubs offered by venerable Grgich Hills Cellars in Rutherford, is a good example; membership runs between $60 and $100 per quarter, depending on the bottles being shipped.

It's not just the Grgich Hills of the world that are offering their most loyal customers such an opportunity. Smaller, younger wineries have wine clubs too. Fiddlehead Cellars, which produces only about 5,000 cases a year from its FiddleHeadquarters in the up-and-coming Lompoc Wine Ghetto, has three clubs that supply its devotees with a bottle (or three, or six) each of Sauvignon Blanc and Pinot Noir three times a year. Naturally, the more you buy, the greater the discount. Indeed, club membership is one of the few ways for Fiddlehead-heads to stay supplied in Fiddlehead, since the winery's vintages and estate bottlings are not widely distributed.

MULTIPLE-WINERY CLUBS

The second type of wine club is one that mixes and matches a selection of bottles from a number of wineries, then distributes them to club members, usually monthly and at a fixed price. The Sunset Wine Club (sunsetwineclub.com) delivers either two reds or a red and a white to your door monthly. Wines are selected by experts including Karen MacNeil, author of the best-selling *The Wine Bible*, and Sara Schneider, *Sunset* magazine's wine editor and the coauthor of this book. As with a number of other wine clubs, shipments are accompanied by recipes for dishes that go well with the month's wines so club members can create food-and-wine-pairing menus for family and friends. Unlike any other club, however, the Sunset Wine Club has its recipes vetted in the fabled Sunset Test Kitchen.

WAITING LISTS

Of course, there are some wineries whose wines are so revered and sought after that even being a member of a club is not enough to get your hands on a bottle. Take Williams Selyem: This Russian River Valley winery is best known for its Pinot Noirs, which grace the wine lists of restaurants like Spago and French Laundry but cannot be found on the racks of your local wine shop. In fact, the only way to be granted the privilege of paying $30 to $70 for a bottle of Williams Selyem Pinot is to go to the winery's website (williams selyem.com), get on the waiting list, and, well, wait. The current backlog is about a year. Once you have endured this rite of patience, you will receive a notice detailing the "projected allocation" of bottles you have been approved to buy, which would be good news were it not for the fact that Williams Selyem is a strictly first-come-first-serve operation, so the day you get your allocation you'd better be ready to write a check. In fact, you'd better be ready to purchase as much of your allocation as your child's college fund can stand, because from that day forward, especially for the next critical couple of years, your buying habits will be monitored to determine if your allocation should be increased in volume and/or broadened in variety—the more you buy, the better your chances of both. If all this sounds a bit much, consider this: The wine is absolutely and unequivocally worth it, and the current owners of the winery began their pursuit of Williams Selyem Pinot Noir by putting their names on the previous owner's list.

INDEX

Amusement park, 98–99
Antiques, 40, 93
Aquarium/marine life
    center, 99, 102, 105,
    108, 141
Art, 9, 12, 14, 15, 18, 20, 22,
    24, 28, 29, 30, 75, 80,
    121, 124, 132

Ballooning, 14
Beach, 91, 98, 101, 117, 124,
    141, 144, 145, 154
Bed & breakfast, 16, 63, 78,
    80, 89, 101, 110, 129,
    149, 150, 155
Beer, 70, 71, 79
Biking, 24, 31, 38, 99, 155
Biodynamic farming, 18,
    23, 40, 48, 67, 68, 74
Boardwalk, 98
Boating, 72
Bocce, 41, 120, 126
Bullfighting, 153

Cabins/cottages, 30, 32,
    33, 43, 44, 45, 70, 75, 98,
    101, 144, 145
Camping, 30, 37, 58, 98, 101
Canoeing, 37, 58, 75
Casino, 149
Cave, 20, 21, 23, 27, 29, 38, 40,
    86, 88, 114, 120, 152, 153
Classes, cooking, 18, 30, 70
Classes, wine, 14, 22, 27, 52
Coastal drive, 34, 108
Conference facility, 148
Croquet, 10, 33, 126
Cruise, 15, 141, 154
Crush, 22, 136
Cultural center, 14, 65, 154

Events, 66

Farmer's market, 14, 15,
    30, 50, 74, 128
Festival, 120, 124
Festival, film, 74
Fishing bait, 50, 72
Fishing, 73, 144, 154, 155
Food-wine pairing, 7, 12, 13,
    22, 23, 40, 46, 52
Funicular, 100

Garden, 11, 14, 20, 25, 30,
    41, 42, 48, 49, 51, 52, 54,
    56, 74, 86, 110, 115, 120,
    122, 133, 134, 140, 144
Garden, sculpture, 11, 106
Golf, 17, 95, 102, 111, 144,
    149, 154
Grappa, 153

Hiking, 30, 31, 41, 42, 43,
    78, 99, 108, 115, 145, 155
Horseback riding, 43, 144,
    155

Jeep tour, 144
Judgment of Paris, 4–5, 10,
    12, 17, 20, 23, 29, 93, 95

Kayaking, 58, 108, 141,
    144, 151, 154

Lake, 14, 29, 72, 73, 130
Lighthouse, 99
Lodging, 10, 16–17, 25,
    32–33, 37, 44–45, 51, 59,
    71, 73, 75, 81, 84–85, 101,
    110–111, 113, 115, 117,
    118, 122, 123, 125, 129,
    132, 144–145, 149, 155
London, Jack, 37, 42

Market, 24, 44, 48, 51, 89,
    120, 138
Mine tour, 84
Mission, 34, 43, 105, 108,
    110, 115, 128, 140, 141
Movie theater, 99
Museum, art and/or
    culture, 42, 62, 70, 82,
    86, 99, 105, 113, 140, 141
Museum, winemaking, 11,
    22, 24
Music, live, 15, 28, 45, 71, 72,
    75, 84, 86, 91, 95, 111, 148

Nature preserve/reserve, 14,
    34, 43, 58, 98

Opera, 15
Orchard, 23, 58, 70, 74, 79,
    80, 81, 140
Organic, 14, 23, 31, 40, 49,
    52, 62, 63, 67, 68, 71, 82,
    106, 125, 136

Outdoor dining, 11, 15, 16,
    20, 22, 32, 38, 40, 41, 44,
    50, 52, 65, 67, 68, 97, 106,
    109, 120, 134, 136, 139,
    142, 147, 148, 149

Park, 24, 30, 31, 42, 43, 77, 78,
    81, 98, 99, 105, 108, 111,
    113, 115, 140
Picnic spots, 11, 23, 24, 28,
    29, 30, 38, 41, 48, 54, 67,
    68, 79, 80, 82, 96, 97, 98,
    106, 120, 121, 126, 133,
    134, 142, 149

Rafting, 78, 81
Ranch, 75, 99, 111, 144, 145
Restaurant, 10, 14, 15–16,
    17, 24–25, 26, 27, 31–32,
    37, 43–44, 50–51, 55,
    58–59, 63, 65, 70–71, 73,
    74, 75, 80, 81, 84, 88,
    89, 95, 99, 100–101, 106,
    108, 109, 111, 113, 115,
    118, 122, 123, 124–125,
    128, 129, 132, 134,
    142–143, 145, 146, 148,
    149, 154, 155
Ruta del Vino, 152

Scuba/snorkel, 151, 154
Shopping, 15, 29, 30, 31, 37,
    38, 42, 49, 59, 98, 99, 101,
    128, 134, 135, 154
Spa, 17, 25, 30, 33, 45, 58,
    70, 89, 101, 144, 148, 155
Spelunking, 88
Steamboat, 75
Steinbeck, John, 102, 113
Surfing, 90, 99
Swimming pool, 17, 25, 30,
    44, 71, 81, 145, 155

Tennis, 145
Theater, 15, 140
Train, 15, 88, 98
Tram, 29

Vegetarian cuisine, 155

Waterskiing, 72, 75
Whale watching, 141, 154
Wine auction, 8
Wine clubs, 158–159